THE NIGHT HE SAVED ME

Saved by Love Series

SARAH STEVENS

THE NIGHT HE SAVED ME
Sarah Stevens Copyright © 2019

Cover Designer:Melissa Gill Designs
Photographer: Lindee Robinson
Photography Cover Models: JJ Butts and Meagan Pacholski Editor: Librum Artis
Editorial Services
Formatter: Jamie Davis

ISBN-13: 978-0692740378
ISBN-10: 0692740376

For Steve, my brother. I love and miss you every day.
Until we meet again.

Huggies and Kisses,
Sarah

LOT'S OF "HUGGIES AND KISSES'
STEVE.

Prologue

I have broken my promise to myself—a promise I wouldn't go down the wrong path.

I hate life here. I didn't sign on to live in a new town, to live in a house I would never consider my own.

Mom and I moved to Maine from New Hampshire a few years ago. My brother stayed behind and is in jail—again, for the hundredth time since he turned 18—and we're living in a quiet suburb of Portland, Maine. My dad left when I was little. He still sends a card here and there, usually when he needs to send a check for a holiday or birthday, and he's paying for my school this year, but Otherwise I hardly see him. Half the time he makes plans to see me and never shows up. It's been just Mom and me until she started dating this guy last year. Me being the rebellious teenager, I don't like it, and I make it known whenever possible. It was supposed to be just Mom and me. I don't need a stepfather, but it looks like I'm getting one anyway. I know mom deserves to be happy, but what about my happiness? And because I've been "one hell of a teenager" lately, things have changed this year, including a new school.

This is the first day of my senior year of high school and *check this out*: I get to go to an all-girls' school. *What the heck did I do to deserve this crap?* Oh yeah, piss off my mom.

After taking a shower, I put on the uniform that the boys think is sexy and I think is a curse before I do my hair and makeup—just a touch of mascara and lip gloss—and then wait for my ride to a school that is in the city, with someone my mom recruited to bring me. I hate life here in the 'burbs.

Why did we come to this place? Why did we sell that house and every childhood memory I had? I miss New Hampshire. I miss my brother. I may be seventeen, but I'm smart enough to realize things will be changing this next year. I just don't know if it's good or bad changes.

Mom thought she was saving me from my brother's life—from the heartbreak the drugs and the alcohol brought upon our family—but I saw; I saw it all. Moving to another state, to a new house, won't take away the memories of the old house, my old life.

Mom has already left for work, so I go back to my room and grab the bottle I have hidden under my bed and take a swig before heading outside to wait for my ride to this godawful school full of girls. Heck, I don't even think at orientation I saw a male teacher in the building—I think even the janitor is a female. I swing my backpack over my shoulder and grab that small rectangular box out of my purse and head around the back of the house for a quick cigarette. When I have a few minutes of peace and a smoke, things don't seem so bad for a moment.

Chapter One

NEW BEGINNINGS

Katarina

It has been a long year.

Junior/Senior prom is right around the corner, and I have finally started to fit in with a group of girls—one in particular, Brenda, who everyone calls Bren. I am sitting in algebra class, the last class of the day, when Bren looks over to me and says, "Hey, Kat, have you ever been in town after school?"

"No, my mom usually wants me to head straight home, with the ride she's arranged for me."

"Hop on the bus and head into town with me. Tell your mom you need to go to the library for a project or something," she suggests.

Once the last bell rings, I head to my locker to call my mom. Thankfully, because it is school related, she says she will pick me up after work at the library.

I look over at Bren, "We're all set, but I have to meet my mom at five at the library to get picked up."

"*Awesome.* Let's go grab the bus," Bren says, beaming.

I had a feeling I was about to walk into a world I had never experienced before. I may drink a shot here and there and smoke a cigarette now and again, but Bren seems to have something different in mind. I see it with the devious look she shoots my way as we walk to the bus stop. I think I know Bren, but I have a feeling I will learn more today about who Bren really is, the one that not a lot of people get to see. I have known Bren this entire year, but this is the first time she's invited me anywhere with her.

Once we make it downtown and jump off the bus, Bren instantly lights up a cigarette, and I follow suit. We head on down to the Old Port and to the park, where Bren makes a beeline for a group of teenagers. Everyone is dressed in normal clothes, and I feel conspicuous in my school uniform. These kids are obviously from the city public school, and some even look like they are a bit older. I notice a few of the girls have piercings in places I couldn't even imagine getting pierced; torn up jeans and tattoos peek out from the shirt sleeves of some of the guys. A few of the kids in the mix even appear as if they may be homeless.

Bren is greeted by everyone here just like she is at school, with hugs and smiles. I don't see how privileged Bren fits in with this motley group, but she does, and they seem to love her. Today, those greetings are followed by a "Who's your girl?"

Who am I?

Well, up until recently, I was a shy girl who never fit into any one group in particular. I'm the girl who just fades into the background. A girl who comes from a broken family. Dad left early on, leaving my mom to raise my brother and me on her own, working so much that she barely saw us. My brother went in the wrong direction and into a group that was all about the party life. I, on the other hand, became the girl who was quiet and enjoyed books over people. Moving to Maine without my brother, it was just mom and me all the time, then she met Kyle, and I was again left home alone more and more. Until I met Bren and she took me under her wing, I was a

4

nothing, with no life experiences. I resent my mom's boyfriend for taking her away from me and I resent my brother for caring more about drugs and his friends than his own family. I'm a loner.

We make the rounds, and she introduces me to this other world she moves in so effortlessly. She seemed like nothing more than the popular girl, living a good, happy life. But I guess we all have our secrets. We all sit in a circle, and the pipe starts making its way through the group. You know, one of those one-hitter pipes for smoking pot that fit in your pocket and are easy to conceal? Yeah, I didn't know what one was until today—like I said, naive.

When it gets to Bren, she takes a hit and then looks at me with brows raised, the unspoken question clear.

Do I? I think to myself. *Yeah, sure, just one. One hit won't kill me, right?* I nod my head at Bren. I have been watching everyone, and it should be easy—inhale, hold, exhale. So, I do, and, of course, even though I smoke, I still look like a fool when I cough up a lung. Yeah, the first day in this new world, and I look like a fool. *Go me.*

The group smokes the rest of the weed then we light up cigarettes and chill. Some guys pull out a hacky sack and start kicking it around; a couple other people pull out guitars and start singing. It is a very Woodstock kind of atmosphere—from what I know of Woodstock, that is.

Bren and I are sitting there talking when I look up across the park and notice someone I hadn't been introduced to, someone not exactly with this crowd. He's dressed more for business, with dark jeans and indigo blue collared shirt. His smile catches my attention, he seems so happy and carefree. It adds a little crinkle around his eyes making his eyes smile too. He has dark-blond hair that hangs in his eyes a bit, and he's tall and lean. This guy is hanging out with some friends, not paying attention to me or anyone else around him, just sipping a coffee. I'm frozen in place, watching his movements, and don't even notice Bren tapping on my shoulder to get my attention.

"Hey, Kat! Kat, Earth to Kat," she says with a chuckle to her voice.

"Huh, what?"

"Hey, girlie, we have to get you back up to the library, and I need to catch my bus to my house. What grabbed your attention and put you in a daze? You okay?"

"Yeah, I'm fine. It was nothing; I was just lost in thought."

We pick our bags up and make the rounds, saying goodbye to the new group of people I can tell will become a refuge from my tedious world. We get up to the library and Bren has to run to catch her bus, so we quickly hug our farewells. "Today was fun, thanks for the invite!"

"We'll have to do it more often. It is a great escape from reality," says Bren as she turns around and jogs toward the bus stop.

About five minutes later, my mom pulls up to the front of the library, and I toss my stuff in the back and climb in. She doesn't say much, just the normal Mom questions.

"How was school?"

"Did you get all your work done?"

I answer them with the normal teenage answers.

"Fine."

"Yes."

Here I go, back into the world I didn't choose, the one that has my mother marrying Kyle in a matter of months. I think it is time for me to choose what I want out of life since eighteen is just a couple of months away.

Over the past few weeks, I have managed to escape at least once a week with Bren to the Old Port with no real issues on the parental end. Each week, I get more and more familiar with the group and the pipe. It feels good to be me for a little while; at least, I think this is me. Each week, I also get to see that mysterious guy with eyes that smile and dark-blond, floppy hair. More recently, I have noticed how nice his body is. This guy is sexy as hell, but just doesn't seem to be a part of this group—he hangs on the periphery, included but not really participating. The way he dresses, the way he acts...he just doesn't seem to fit the mold of this group of people.

Tonight, I have managed to get away for the entire night. I told my mom that Bren invited me to spend the night at her house, and Bren told her mom that she's spending the night at my house. *Ha!* Parents are so gullible. You'd think with my brother always in jail, my mom would have figured out when she was being played. Good thing I have always been the angel in the family, the one that until recently could do no wrong.

We actually *do* go to Bren's house for a bit after school. Two weeks ago, for Bren's birthday, her mom and dad surprised her with a brand new, silver Honda Civic. We no longer have to take the bus on our excursions, which means we have a whole new level of freedom at our fingertips.

We get to her house, and while her parents are still at work, we start getting ready for the party tonight. Thankfully, I am not much bigger than Bren, so her clothes tend to fit me, and let me tell you, her choice of clothes is so much better than my wardrobe at home, where my mom still thinks I am a child who is good with the typical Maine look of jeans and a flannel. At least I have some cute shoes, right?

With an hour of Bren's touches complete, I look like a new girl. My long, dark, frizzy hair is now sleek, and I have sculpted curls that hang perfectly around my shoulders. My face—*oh my God*, I have never seen my face look this way. Mom says no makeup, except for mascara and gloss, and Bren has made me reconsider my mother's opinion. Let's just hope she can teach me how to use it once I buy some.

I feel beautiful. I feel like a new person, and I think I have gained some confidence just by looking different. We leave her house to grab some dinner and then make our way downtown to where Bren was told the party is at. One of her friends invited us to the party at his apartment just outside the Old Port. Everyone recognizes Bren, and I hear the same thing I heard when I first started hanging out with her.

"Hey, Bren. Who's your girl?"

We look at each other and laugh. I can't believe my girl transformed me so much that no one recognizes me! Bren and I walk around, and as I get re-introduced, I get offered hit after hit from everyone's bowl or joint. I take a hit off some and pass on the others.

After grabbing a drink for the both of us, I follow Bren to the roof deck for some fresh air. It was getting hard to breathe in that small space, the smoke making the air heavy and thick with haze. I could hardly see two feet in front of me. I sure as hell couldn't hear a thing that Bren was saying over the loud music and people talking and laughing.

We still hear the music when we get outside, but at least we don't have to yell at each other to be heard. A group of guys—I think their names are Damon, Jon, and Nate—are gathered at a table at the end of the deck. Once we step closer to the table, I realize what I just walked up on: white powder, glass table, and rolled-up bills. This is where I have to decide if I ignore what they are doing or join in. When I glance over to Bren, I realize she is giving me that look again. The unspoken question.

I've had quite a few hits of weed with her since arriving and started drinking when we made our way out here, and now I am faced with this. *Well, shit, what the hell.* You only live once, and this is a night to remember. *I hope.*

I take the bill after Bren has made two perfectly-straight lines on the table and snorted hers. *Okay, I can do this.*

Close one nostril.

Put the bill in the other.

Inhale the white powder—the entire line.

Drop the bill, head back, and keep inhaling it through my nasal passage.

I feel the burn as it is sucked through my nasal passage, and then I taste it in the back of my throat. For the next half hour, I am sniffling like I have a cold and tasting the drip, but honestly, after the first few minutes, I don't care. I am feeling no pain; I haven't felt this light and free since ...well...ever, and I watch the world go by with my best friend next to me. As I sit on one of the lounge chairs set up on the roof next to Bren, looking into the night, I think of my brother. *This is one night.* Just one night. I *am not* an addict like he is. One time won't kill me.

Later, in the night, things become chill as everyone has had their share of pot, the cocaine effects have worn off and drinks are still flowing. The music is still blaring through the speakers and everyone is yelling to be heard over it. I look around and realize Bren is nowhere to be found—she has left me sitting there on the couch against the wall on the far side of the room. I don't mind because I am enjoying my buzz. The next thing I know, this really cute guy sits next to me and starts talking. No biggie, right? I have all the confidence in the world. Who cares if a guy has never talked to me before and has never shown any interest in me? My confidence at an all-time high from my new look and the euphoria of the drugs, I sit and talk to him. Finally, I get his name—was it Nick, Trent? God, I can't get his name right.

The talking has stopped; he is kissing all over my neck, pulling me closer and working his way up to my mouth. *God, he's cute.* In a matter of minutes, I am on his lap, the world around me long forgotten. For once, I feel special. And then things start to change. I have lost all control of myself. My head is spinning, and I am starting to realize that the mix of tonight's activities was *so* not a good idea. I should have stuck to one thing, whether it be the pot, the booze, or the coke. I feel present—I know what is going on—but my body won't move the way I tell it to. Before I can react, my body is being forced down on the couch, my skirt is flipped up, and my panties are ripped away from my body. My arms are too heavy—I feel like I weigh a million pounds when I try to shove him away from me, which he deflects without a bit of effort.

I yell at him to stop, and I try to kick him away, but I can't; the drugs have consumed my body, and I feel so weighed down. He doesn't seem to care that I don't want this to happen; he is going to do this to me anyway, and that is evident when he shoves his dick inside me. I scream out in pain as tears run down my face, but no one is hearing me over the music. He covers my mouth anyway and keeps going. The pain is blinding. I try to push him away again, but grief and pain and fear leave me almost paralyzed. I have just lost myself.

I am no longer whole.

∽♡∾

James Russo

I stand there, where I do every day at this time, but this day is different. *She* is different—innocent and beautiful. She doesn't belong in this environment, with all the smoking and drugs.

I continue playing a game of hacky sack with my friends. I go about my game but notice she keeps looking in my direction. I try to ignore her, but she is a beautiful girl. Dark, curly hair and a fair complexion. When I get closer, I notice her bright-blue eyes. *I'm going to be in trouble.*

I finish my game with my friends, and then it's time to make my way back down the street to The Java. This place has become my baby—the thing I live for. Ever since I was old enough to make my own decisions, I knew I wanted my own life, not one that was dictated by my family. After my parents passed away, I discovered my dad wasn't really my dad, and my biological father wanted me under his thumb. I did everything I could to separate from him, so I came here and opened up my coffee shop, The Java. I like the life I'm living now, the freedoms I'm allowed.

I walk away but take a second to glance back toward her. She is surrounded by the park kids, and she is too innocent to be around them. God, I want to go grab her up and take her away from that world, but I don't. I feel the need to protect her, like it's my responsibility, and I don't know why. I turn around and head in the direction of The Java, back to the world that I have made mine. As I walk down the street, I wonder if she'll be back. I hope so; I have to see her again even, if it is from a distance. But those eyes, they caught me off guard. I'd do anything to look directly into them, just a moment to see a glimpse of her soul. I keep walking and make it to the door, this mystery girl still on my mind. *Damn, when did I become so wrapped up in a girl, especially one who I don't have a name for, one so innocent, so young? I think I just might be screwed.*

As I walk into The Java I'm greeted by my staff, the aroma of coffee invading my nose. I love that smell.

Jayce, my day manager, takes one look at me and raises his brows. "Dude, what's going on? You all right, man?"

"Yeah, I'm good," I reply. "Just a bit on my mind." He hands me my usual latte, and I walk to my office. *Yeah, I'm screwed; I've got to meet her.*

She is stuck in my head after just a glimpse.

Chapter Two

Katarina

I need to get out of here before anyone notices something is wrong with me. Bren is my ride, so after I clean myself up in the bathroom, I set off to find her. I look normal, but I don't feel normal. Not anymore. And no one will ever know the truth of what I just experienced. We went, we partied, and I went home. *End of story.*

The next day, I walk in the door and am greeted by my mom. "How was your night, sweetie?"

"Great!" I reply, hoping I look normal even if I feel anything but. Should I tell her what happened? Should I have at least told Bren? Maybe I should have gone to the police, but who's going to believe a girl who was completely trashed and can't even tell you the first name of the person who raped her? "We had a late night, Mom, so I'm going to go take a shower and get a nap. Then I have to get my homework done. Call me when dinner's ready."

I walk toward my room, get undressed, throw my clothes away, and get into the hottest shower I have ever had. It's too much—

everything I am feeling—and I crash. Tears start to stream down my face as I sit there in the shower, reliving my nightmare. All of a sudden, I feel panicked. Grabbing my puff, I douse it with soap and start scrubbing every inch of my body. There is no escape—this feeling won't go away. I scrub and sob and scrub some more. Nothing is helping, so I sit there until the water runs cold and I'm shivering. Finally, I step out of the shower, wrap myself in my soft fluffy towel, and crawl in bed. My bed, a safe place—or so I thought.

About an hour into my nap, I wake myself up with the nightmare that won't go away. I didn't even realize I was crying. Sleep at this point is hopeless, so I get up and snatch my backpack off the floor. *Guess I'll start my homework until dinner time.*

Next thing I know, my homework is complete, and Mom is calling me for dinner.

"I'll be right there," I shout back then head toward the bathroom to take a look at myself. Yeah, bad idea there; I look like shit. My eyes are swollen and dull, and my face is blank, like I feel nothing. I'm numb. *Time to use some acting skills I learned in drama class and put on a happy face for Mom.*

I head off to the kitchen to see what's for dinner, and Mom looks at me, a weird look crossing her face for a moment, then looks at Kyle. *Can she tell something is wrong with me?* Spread out on the table is my favorite meal: Shepherd's pie made the traditional way, with biscuits on the side. I'm almost afraid to ask what is going on here. She never makes this meal anymore unless something serious is going on. The last few times she's made it was to tell me we were leaving our home in New Hampshire, and then to tell me she and Kyle were getting married. *What is going on now?* I better not have to move from this house; I was just starting to like it here.

It doesn't take long for her to open her mouth. "Sweetie, we have to tell you something."

"I knew something was going on when you made this," I tell her, pointing to my plate.

"Well, sweetie, Kyle and I will be married soon, and we have decided what we are going to do about living arrangements after we are married."

"*I knew it.* I refuse to move again, Mom."

"I'm sorry," she says. "This house isn't big enough for us all."

"We have to combine into one house, Kat. Your mom and I can't live like we have been. We both work, and it would be nice to have my wife by my side at night," Kyle adds.

"Why can't you move into this house, Kyle? Why do we have to be uprooted again?"

"I'm really getting tired of this spoiled brat attitude you keep dishing out, Kat. When are you going to realize I make your mom happy? I'd like to make you happy, too, if you would just give me that chance."

"Here's your chance: I don't want to move. But while we're on the subject, don't bother trying to make me happy. You aren't my dad, and you never will be."

"At least I'm here." Kyle spits back at me. My mom shoots him a murderous look. "Shit, I'm sorry. I shouldn't have said that."

Ignoring the asshole Kyle, I announce, "I'm *not* moving." *A bit immature, but it is how I feel.*

"You don't have a choice; the decision has been made," Mom fires back at me.

"Yeah, and without me, thanks a lot. I get it, and I'm done with it all."

Pushing back from the table, I run to my room and call Bren and ask her to come get me. I can't deal with this shit on top of what happened last night. I feel like I'm going to explode into a million tiny pieces. I need to feel *nothing*. Bren will help me there.

Bren shows up in a matter of twenty minutes, and I'm out the door with a slam that rattles the windows. Bren takes one look at me, and she knows I am about to combust, and I do.

"She is moving me out of my house and into his. I can't go; I won't go. I fuckin' hate this shit. Why can't they wait a few more months until the end of summer? I'll be eighteen then and can make my own decisions. College will be right around the corner and I won't have to worry about where my mom is living. I don't have a license yet, or a car, and I'll never see anyone anymore. I just can't do it.

She looks over at me once we stop at the light, smirks at me, and lights up a joint.

"Try this, K, I think it might help."

I take it from her, and have a flash of doubt about hitting it, after what transpired last night. Weed isn't so bad, I reason. I'm with Bren, and it's just a hit. It will help take the edge off, so I inhale, hold it in, and release. *Yeah, this will work; I knew Bren would help me out.*

"Feel better?" she asks with a knowing look on her face.

"Yeah, I do, thanks. I needed that."

"Great party last night, huh?" she asks me.

I once again have that panicked feeling and toss on my fake smile before I say, "Yeah, it was. Where are you taking me?"

"Some place you will have fun, I promise."

"Sounds great." I inwardly cringe. I was supposed to have fun last night and it became my worst nightmare. Maybe I should tell her what happened, put a little trust in my best friend. But I don't. I just can't find the words.

We pull up to a building—once again a place I've never been to—and walk up three flights of stairs to a seemingly new apartment filled with people, drinks, and weed. *Just a little weed,* I tell myself. *Nothing else.* As the hours go by, I'm getting higher and higher, and the terrible feelings inside me ease. Then I see *him*. He is standing there with a smirk on his face, looking right at me. He knows what he did to me, and I can't be here a minute more—my nightmare is staring at me from across the room. I panic and scramble to find Bren.

"Hey, girl, I gotta get going; it's getting late. Are you cool to drive?" I feel a presence behind me, and I fear the worse. *Please don't let it be him.* I slowly turn around and see it thankfully isn't him, but one of the other guys—one of the nice guys we were with last night; I think his name is Jayce. He offers to take me home, says he is straight and can drive. Bren has a look of gratitude on her face, then turns to me asking, "Are you okay to go with Jayce? He's a good guy; we've known each other for years."

"Yeah, as long as you know him, I'm good to get a ride."

Bren hugs me goodbye before returning her attention to the boy she was flirting with. I look at Jayce, a little hesitant to go with him, but it is the only way to get home and I can't stay here.

"You ready to get out of here?" he asks

"Sure, let's go," I agree, still not completely sure about this choice.

We get to his Honda, which looks like it has seen better days, and I direct him toward my home, at least my home for now. Irritation flares within me once more at the thought.

"I really appreciate the ride, Jayce. Thank you."

"I really don't mind. I wanted to get out of there anyway. I have to work tomorrow at The Java in Old Port. You should come check it out sometime," he says with a wink.

"I will next time I am down there. So, how old are you, anyway? Seems like the crowd tonight was older then what Bren usually takes me to."

"I'm eighteen, almost nineteen."

"Not too much older. Hey, turn here, and can you please park in front of that blue house? I live a few houses down but my mom won't like me being dropped off in a different car than I was picked up in."

"No problem." Jayce parks the car along the curb, puts it in park, then looks over at me.

He has this hungry look in his eyes. I know he wants to kiss me, and my intuition is confirmed when he starts to lean in my direction. He makes contact with my lips briefly. His lips are soft, for the brief second of contact, but I pull back, a hint of panic already rising within me.

Pulling back, I say, "I'm sorry. I can't do this. You're nice, but I just don't feel it."

He has a look of disappointment on his face but nods. "It's okay. I thought I'd at least try. You're beautiful and sweet. I like you."

"I just can't. I'm sorry, I've got to go." I get out and head for my house, hoping Mom isn't awake. *Yeah, no such luck.*

"Where have you been?" she hollers in my direction, coming out of her bedroom.

"Out with Bren. We hung out at a friend's house."

"You reek of pot, Kat—have you been smoking? "Her volume is rising on every word, and I can't stop my mouth.

"So, what if I have? You don't seem to care what's good for me these days, just what's good for you."

"How dare you, young lady!" Her palm flies across my face and I jerk back, unable to stop the tears filling my eyes.

"I'm done! Leave me alone. Go be with Kyle," I spit, taking off for my room.

"Get back here!" she shouts after me.

Not caring what she thinks, I slam my bedroom door and lock it, falling onto my bed.

Why is every day the worst day ever?

〜

James

Another day and no sign of her. *Where is she? Is she okay? Why am I even asking myself these questions?* I have seen her friend, the tall one with dark hair, but no sign of her. *Do I dare ask her about her friend? What is wrong with me?*

It has been over a week, almost two and I don't even know why I care. Seriously, she has to be too young for me. As a matter of fact, I know she is, because she was wearing a school uniform the first time I saw her. I've seen her at least once a week over the past month here, but this week...nothing. I head back to The Java and am greeted by Jayce and my afternoon latte.

"Hey, Jayce, how goes it today?"

"It's going great; business is good today."

"Awesome, I'm headed to my office if you need me for anything."

"Got it, boss."

Turning toward my office, I am overwhelmed with an odd sensation. When I hear the door open behind me and I hear her voice, my body hums with anger, —truthfully, I'm jealous, an emotion I have no right to, considering I don't even know this girl, but I feel ghosted.

"Hey, Jayce, how are ya? Since you told me about this place, I had to grab Bren and come check it out."

"Hey, Kat, what are you doing in town today? Bren told me you were having some trouble with the parental unit."

"Yeah, life has totally sucked at home. Mom didn't like the fact I took off and that it was you, or at least not Bren, that brought me home. Apparently, she saw your car dropping me off even though I thought we were out of view. Also, she didn't appreciate my smelling like weed."

"Yeah, well, I'm glad to see your pretty face again. Sorry if I made things worse bringing you home the other night."

"Yeah, about that, are we good? I like you, but I just can't right now."

"We're fine. I figured I would take a shot when I had the chance. It didn't go as I planned, but at least I got to kiss you."

Bren pipes in with a slightly offended tone. "He kissed you? Why didn't you tell me?"

Kat ignores Bren and continues. "Yeah, no shame in your technique, Jayce, but I'd rather be friends right now while I have some shit going on."

"It is all good, K, what can I get you and Bren? I got this one for you both."

"Caramel macchiato would hit the spot," says Bren.

"I guess the same for me too," Kat says.

"You got it!"

Hiding in my own place to hear a conversation between the girl that has me crazy and the guy who works for me, I instantly feel like a total creep. I don't like what I am hearing. It has my blood boiling, but why? She isn't mine, and she doesn't even know that I exist. So, I do what I shouldn't do and turn toward the counter and give Jayce a hard time.

"Jayce, you giving away my drinks now?"

"Hey, boss," replies Jayce. "Yeah, just this once, to this girl who won't say yes to me. And one for her friend."

"Ah, I see. You're trying to *woo* the girl."

"Dude, who says woo anymore?"

"Eh, it sounded good. Who are your friends?"

"James, this is my friend, Kat, and her friend, Bren. Kat and Bren, this is the boss, James."

I look at her, directly into her eyes, and hold my hand out. "Nice to meet you, Kat."

She looks at me, frozen for a second. I caught it, but I don't think anyone else did. "Hi, nice to meet you, James." Her complexion flushes a red so bright you would think she had spent hours in the sun as she shakes my hand.

"Well, ladies, it was nice to meet you, but I have to get back to the office. Enjoy your lattes and have a great day."

"Nice to meet you too," Kat says. With a quick nod of my head, I turn on my heel and head back toward the office once more. At least I don't feel like such a creep anymore, considering I clearly affect this beautiful girl as much as she affects me. I still have this problem of her being a high school student. I just wish I understood why I am so drawn to her, because we haven't even had a real conversation yet. Her beauty just pulls me in.

Today was a good day.

Chapter Three

Katarina

I met him. Oh, my *God,* I met him. His eyes are so much better up close, and that smile, or should I say smirk—perfection!

After Bren and I left The Java, we went back to the park to catch up to our friends. I have been MIA for over a week now, and I missed some of them—not all, but some. I give hugs to the ones I like and just say hi to the ones that I think are all right, then I see *him,* and I freeze. He is staring right at me again, like he did at the party the other night.

I look over at Bren and let her know that my time here is up. Ever since I left the house without a word to my mother, I have been on a short leash; I'm lucky I was even allowed to "go to the library" at all this week.

I head up the street to the library and make it within minutes of my mom's arrival to pick me up. I really am not interested in going home, but alas, I have to. Prom is coming up in a few weeks, and even though I don't have a date, I still want to go. Bren and her date are going to come pick me up on their way. I have the perfect dress picked out—a beautiful, deep purple Jovani, with a strapless top and a flowing, tulle bottom. I also got these amazing, matching strappy shoes with rhinestone accents.

I am so excited for this night to come, and everything is planned. I just have to follow the rules for a few more weeks. Unfortunately, by following the rules, it also means I have to help my mom pack on the weekends for the big move after her honeymoon. Prom is three weeks away, and the wedding five. *Oh, what joy.* At least I have one amazing thing to look forward to, though having a date would make it so much better.

♡

The weeks fly by. In that time, I have managed to go the library twice, and that also means I have been able to see James in those two visits, as well as Jayce. I feel bad; he is a sweet guy; I just don't have any romantic feelings for him. The last time I saw Jayce, he asked me about prom and if I had a date. We all know that answer, so I was honest.

"I sure don't."

"Do you want a date?"

"It would be nice but not necessary. Bren and her date are planning on picking me up."

"Would you like me to be your date, as a friend?"

I looked over to Bren and saw that look on her face—she set this up. Bren wanted me to have a date, and she wants me to get together with Jayce.

"Um, do you have a tux?"

"I can get one if I need one."

"Okay. As long as we are going just as friends."

I held my hand out to shake on it

"Friends."

Here we go. I have a date now! I was set up and I know it, and as much as

I am not attracted to him, I am so much more excited because I won't be a third wheel.

So, for the next five minutes, we nailed down the plans, and then James walked in. I was embarrassed by the way he made me feel, but that didn't stop my heart from racing or my face from turning the color of a ripe tomato.

"Hey, girls, how are you today?"

"Great," Bren replied. *"K just got a date to prom with our boy Jayce here."*

"Oh, yeah? that's good." Something about his tone made me glance back his way. His jaw was tight and his teeth were clenched.

"Yeah we are going as friends," I said, narrowing my eyes at Jayce.

"I tried, she just won't go for my charm and go on a non-friend date with me."

James's face relaxed marginally. "Sucks to be you! Oh, and get back to work, slacker," he teased as he walked back to his office.

Jayce got up, said his goodbyes, and moved behind the counter. I looked at the time and panicked. I had literally two minutes to get to the library for my pick-up, and it usually took five minutes to get there on a good day.

"Shit! I gotta go, Bren; I'm late to meet my mom!"

"Crap, I lost track of time too," she said, jumping up. We both went bolting out the door.

Apparently, it was my lucky day; my mom was five minutes late, so when I got there she was nowhere to be seen. I took a seat to catch my breath. When I looked up, I saw him—my nightmare. He seemed to follow me wherever I go. He looked straight into my eyes and held my stare. Why does he keep staring at me and showing up everywhere? Is he following me? Just then, my mom rolled up and honked the horn to get my attention. I jumped in, for once relieved to see her.

James

Prom, with Jayce? *I have a damn problem here.* She looked at me straight in the eyes, saw my reaction—my jaw clenching—and quickly made sure that I knew there was nothing going on. *Why would she do that? Does she know what she does to me?* She is in my head all day and all night, and I can't get her out. I need to let this thing go, to let thoughts of her go. She's too young, I try to tell myself, but I'm so damn attracted to her. She may almost be eighteen to my twenty-two, but she is still in high school and will want to go to college, live life, and have fun, not getting tied down by someone. Kat doesn't need me in her life, but damn, I wish she was in mine.

I realize how young she really is when she has to bolt out of my place to meet her mom. I shouldn't even let myself think the things I think about her. I huff out a sigh and shake my head.

"You all right, boss? You're not looking so hot," Jayce says.

"Yeah, I'm fine," I reply and start toward my office. I need to get things done and get her out of my head.

I sit there at my desk with her still lingering on my mind. What I really want more than anything is to have a conversation with her, get to know the person underneath the beauty that has drawn me to her.

Chapter Four

Katarina

Prom day has finally come. My nails are painted, my makeup flawless, and my hair perfectly curled with no frizz in sight.

Mom comes into my room with a sparkle in her eye. "Are you excited for tonight, K?" she asks, her voice filled with excitement. For the first time in weeks we are both putting our strained relationship behind us for this night.

"Yeah, Mom, I'm really excited. Bren will be here in about an hour," I remind her.

The afternoon was filled with appointments at two different salons, and I let her know just how long I had to get ready every step of the way.

"Well, you look beautiful," she tells me. "Even without the dress on yet."

"Thanks, Mom. I think I should have listened to you, though. I have way too long to wait for Bren and I'm all ready to go."

"Time will fly. Take a few minutes to breathe, eat a snack, then go put on the dress."

. . .

Times does fly. I am standing there in front of the mirror, dressed to kill in my purple Jovani dress, when the doorbell rings. I jump into action, grab my clutch, apply my lip-gloss, and head toward the front door, hoping it is just Bren at the door. I am so not in the mood for questions from Mom about Jayce and who he is.

No such luck—all three of them are standing there looking like the beautiful people they are as I stand there feeling six inches tall.

My mom looks at me and says, "Come here, K, you look stunning. I need to grab the camera and get some pictures before you all take off."

Surprisingly enough, she is too excited about prom to ask questions, so I escape that as she starts taking pictures and blinding us with her flash.

"*Mom*, we need to go, are you done taking pictures now?"

"Fine, party pooper, I'm done," she says. As we head out of the door, she yells, "Have fun and be safe!"

Finally free of my house, we are headed off for the night, but before I know it, I have a joint in my face.

Jayce looks at me with a smirk on his face. "Want some?"

"Sure, just a hit or two."

Soon, we are high and stopping at The Java. "Why are we here?"

"I need a latte, anyone else? Come on, K, let's go in."

Both Bren and her date are too busy in the back seat to even notice we stopped. Always the popular party girl that gets the guy, I think to myself. There is no answer from them, so we head on out after we snag a parking spot out front to get a couple lattes. When we walk in, the first thing I notice are those eyes—those bright blue eyes—behind the counter, and they are staring right back at me.

"Hey, boss, can we get a couple lattes?" Jayce is grinning, clearly enjoying this moment on the other side of the counter.

"Sure," replies James.

"Kat, what do you want?"

"Um, I guess I will take something with caramel. I usually don't get anything fancy, just a coffee with lots of sugar."

"You got it. Boss, can I get a caramel macchiato for Kat and mocha for myself?"

"Sure, coming right up. You guys are looking pretty polished— heading off to prom?"

I go to reply, but as soon as I open my mouth, Jayce replies for me. For some reason, that infuriates me. It's like I am not even there, almost like Jayce doesn't want me to even talk to James. The question is, why? *Why is he against me talking to his boss? Is he jealous?*

I stand there like I am invisible while Jayce says, "Yeah, we are heading off to Kat's prom. Should be a good time tonight."

The look on his face makes it seem like he is expecting more from me. *What the hell have I gotten myself into?*

"Sounds fun, hope you have a great time," James growls as he hands us our drinks. But the look on his face is doesn't seem to match his words—his jaw is clenched, and it's obvious he has more to say but won't.

Chapter Five

Katarina

Once we get to the hotel where prom is being held, we park the car and walk into the ballroom. It is decorated in light-blue and silver, reminding me of Cinderella's dress. The music is pounding out the latest Taylor Swift song, and we make our way to our friends' table.

I look over to Bren and say, "This is beautiful. I think I'm glad you made me come after all." Once we say hi to our friends and introduce the guys to everyone, we go over to the stereotypical arch to have our official prom pictures taken. Finally, the formalities are over, and we all decide to hit the dance floor. So far, everything is going great; we dance and get punch, then dance some more. As the song ends, we hear the mic being picked up and then the announcements start.

"Welcome to the Greyson/St. Martha's Junior/Senior prom! It is time to announce Prom King and Queen. First off, the prom king. Darren Knight, come get your crown!" Everyone hoots and hollers, and Darren makes his way up to the stage. "Now, for our Queen of the night... Let's welcome Brenda Montgomery to the stage."

Rushing over to Bren, I give her a hug to congratulate her before she goes to grab her crown. I kinda figured she would get it, but I didn't think she actually cared. We stick around a little while longer, watching Bren and Darren have their King and Queen dance under the mirror ball. After her dance, we all dance a while before we decide it is time to go. When we get out to the lobby and start to move to the door, Bren grabs my arm and stops me.

"Hey, there is a party going on tonight at Lucca's, do you want to go?"

"Dressed like this?" I ask.

"Sure, why not? We just went to prom, now it is time for some extracurricular activities. We will just look amazing doing them!"

"I don't know, Bren, I don't really feel like partying like you want to," I reply.

"Just come," she wheedles. "You don't have to do anything you don't want to."

"Bren, every time we go to these parties, you leave me by myself and go off and do your own thing."

"I'm sorry, I haven't really been a great friend to you, lately have I?"

"You could be a little better, especially at these parties you drag me to."

"I promise, from now on I won't leave your side."

"Okay, we can go for a little while, I guess."

We all walk out to the car and make our way to Lucca's apartment, only to find that we aren't the only ones dressed in prom attire. I didn't realize how many people from the brother/sister schools actually were into this scene. This party is no different than the others we have been to lately, but this time I have a date, and Bren said she's stay with me, so I should be safe, right?

Once we settle into the party and find our circle, the joint is being passed around, and then I notice on the table is the glass square and the white powder. Looks like this is going to be an interesting night again. I decide right then and there I will take a couple hits off the joint and maybe a drink but keep the powder away. I don't like the feeling of not being in control of myself, especially after what happened last time. I won't ever let myself get to that point again. Bren is right next to us on the couch with her date beside her. I notice she hasn't touched the powder sitting on the table, and that makes me happy. We're having a chill time.

Things are going fine for the first hour, then Jayce intrudes on my bubble; he is right next to me, thighs touching, and he leans back and wraps his arm around my shoulders, tugging me into his side. He turns his head in my direction with a smirk on his face, like he is proud of himself. I'm just stoned enough at this point that I'm relaxed and comfortable and give in for a second before the panic starts to take over, and I try to pull away. He's acting more like a boyfriend than a friend. He pulls me back into his side and leans his head closer to mine to captures my lips with his. I freeze in place, not wanting this, not wanting *him*. My heart starts beating again and I jerk back from him, getting to my feet and rushing to the door. Behind me, I hear, "K, stop! Don't leave! Where are you going?"

I turn around, look him in the eyes, and say, "Anywhere besides here. I told you *friends*; that's all I want from you is to be *friends*." I turn on my heel and slam the apartment door in his face, as Bren reaches his side to see what was going on. Bolting down the stairs and out the front door, I stop.

"Shit, where am I going to go?"

"Kat, stop. What happened?" Bren had followed me down the stairs.

I have no ride. I look at my phone and notice that it is still kinda early in the night, about 10:30. *I'm close to The Java, and they close at 11:00. I'll go there.*

33

"Jayce happened. He doesn't get it. I don't want that from him," I yell at her.

"Why? He's a great guy. What's stopping you?"

Standing there, the past few weeks run through my head, and I wonder if I should just come out and tell her what happened at the first party. I don't.

"I'm going to The Java. Just go back upstairs, I'll be fine." I turn and start walking down the street, too angry to even care about how I'll get home later.

Chapter Six

Katarina

I stomp down the street in the direction of The Java and make it with twenty minutes to spare before closing. I try to sneak in without him noticing me, but I sure as hell am not successful. Immediately, James makes his way over in my direction with a questioning look on his face.

"I thought you were at prom?"

"I was, and it was fun, but then we went to this party. I got a little high and had a couple of drinks, and then Jayce kissed me."

"He did *what*? I thought you two were going to prom as friends. *Just* friends. Friends don't do that." He sits next to me, a bit tense at first.

"Mmm, that's what I said. It isn't the first time he has kissed me. He took me home one night and pulled the same shit."

James' voice got quieter, almost sweet, when he asked, "Are you okay? Do you want something to drink? What can I do for you?"

I was beginning to realize that the only friend I had around here was James; his voice had such a caring tone to it. I wanted to hug

SARAH STEVENS

him and maybe even cry on his shoulder. I didn't, I just sat there and stared at him with a look of confusion. "Why are you being so nice to me when you don't even know me?"

James looks at me with a weird look on his face. "You remind me of someone I once knew."

"Ah. I don't know what to do. I ran out of the party, Bren came after me and I just told her to go back to the party, I really don't want to call my mom for a ride home. "

"I can take you home, just let me close up here and we can be on the way. Sure you don't want anything to drink while you wait? Maybe something to munch on?" He has a smirk on his face and a knowing look in his eyes—he knows I'm stoned and probably guesses I have the munchies by now.

"Sure, I'm not picky. Whatever you have would be great."

He brings over a blueberry muffin and an Italian soda and doesn't say a word, just takes a seat next to me. For a while, I sit there in silence, eating my muffin and watching him out the corner of my eye.

"Why are you looking at me like that?" I ask when the silence and his stare gets to be a bit much.

He shakes his head like he's coming back to the moment and realizes I've asked him a question.

"Sorry, I wasn't meaning to stare. You look beautiful tonight, by the way."

"Thank you."

"Tell me something about you, Kat. I know you're in high school, and your best friend is Bren, but tell me about you."

"Why?"

"Because right now I think you need a friend, and friends talk, get to know each other."

I sigh. "You're right, I could use a friend right about now, because I have to question how much of a friend Bren is at the moment. Well, I'm a senior at Sr. Martha's, about to turn eighteen, and I love the color blue. What about you, James? Tell me something about you."

"Besides the obvious, I too love the color blue, and I just turned 22 right before we met. I've owned this place for almost a year now and love it. Do you have any brothers or sisters?"

"I have an older brother. He lives in New Hampshire. Mom and I moved here a couple years ago. Last year she met this guy, Kyle, and now they are getting married. Life hasn't gone exactly like I would have wanted it to go lately. I'm planning to go to the university here in Portland this fall with Bren."

"You didn't want to venture too far from home for college?"

"Nah, I like it around here, for the most part. I think the furthest I'd want to go is New Hampshire or Massachusetts. What about you? Any college?"

"I thought about it, but didn't go. I was a little messed up for a while but quickly got my head on straight and started making plans to do this." He waves his hand around him, motioning to the café.

"I like this place. It's comfortable, not your typical chain coffee place."

"Thanks, I like it too." He gives me a look that could burn right through my dress.

I lower my eyes away from his penetrating look as heat crawls up my face and cram the final bite of muffin in my face. "Where do you want me to put this?" I ask, feeling completely off-kilter from the way he is looking at me.

He replies like nothing just happened between us, "I'll take it. I have some other dishes I need to wash before we can get out of here."

Ignoring the heat I just felt, that second of a connection between us, I answer, "Nope, not gonna happen. I'll wash the dishes while you finish up the other stuff you need to do; it's the least I can do for you helping me out tonight."

"What about your dress? I don't want you to get it wet or dirty," he says.

"It's fine, James. I'll do the dishes, and you do whatever else you need to do to clean up." I walk to the back without another word.

As I'm back there doing the dishes, I have some time to process this train wreck of a night. I get done with the dishes, dry my hands, and then think to check my phone, where a text from Bren is waiting for me.

Bren: Are you okay?
Me: Yeah. I'm at The Java.
Me: don't worry I have a ride home
Bren: who?
Me: a friend I ran into
Bren: okay if you're sure
Me: call you tomorrow
Me: Night
Bren: okay night

I feel bad blowing her off, but I am still upset. I know she wants me to be with Jayce, but I can't do it. He is nice, I just can't—not right now. She shouldn't push it when I made it clear to everyone that friendship was all I wanted. *Gah, I need a vacation from this life, like yesterday.* I walk back out to the café at the same time James comes walking out of what I assume is his office.

"Ready?" he asks

"Yeah, I guess I am," I reply.

Then he turns around and starts walking away.

"Um, James, the door is this way."

He chuckles. "I know, Kat, but the back door and my car are this way."

"Oh, right." *I feel like an idiot.*

Finally, we get to his car, and I'm impressed—an Infinity Q50.

This car is perfection: four-door, deep blue, chrome rims. I think I just fell in love for the first time. At the same time, I start to feel like my naïve, shy self again. *I can't believe I am in a car with this guy that I have been long-distance crushing on for so long.*

I start to feel my face get hot, and I thank the stars that it is dark in his car. I think my high is over now, and all I can think about now is how close I am to James. I wish I understood why he was so kind to me, why a seventeen-year-old would hold even a second of his attention. He feels like my knight in shining armor tonight, and I plan on enjoying my time with him.

We get out onto the main street from the alley behind his building, and before he turns, he looks over to me with a questioning look. "Where to?"

Oh, my God, I feel so stupid. "Oh yeah, um head on out to Congress Street. I actually live a bit away from the city. I forgot to tell you I'm over in Falmouth."

"Oh, it's fine, I don't have anywhere else to be. I'd rather make sure you get home and aren't in a place you don't feel right being," he says.

We spend a majority of the drive in comfortable silence as I fall in love even more with his car. Once we start to get close, I give him directions, and then we are in front of my house. "Thanks, James. I appreciate the ride and the place to hang out away from my crazy life."

"No problem, Kat, I'm glad I was there to help you when you needed it."

I lean over and give him a hug. He hesitates for a moment, is stiff in my arms, and then as I am about to release him, he wraps his arms around me and squeezes me back. I really want to kiss him, but I won't. I can't. I don't have the courage to do something that bold, so I enjoy the feel of his hard body for a few seconds before I get out of his car.

"Thanks again."

Chapter Seven

Katarina

It has been a week since I have seen either boy. I have been feeling like total crap all day every day, sick at my stomach and exhausted. I haven't even been able to eat anything besides a bit of a plain bagel and some ginger ale. Something is seriously wrong with me, but I hate going to the doctor, so I decide to text Bren, since she is supposed to stop by anyway with my missed schoolwork.

Me: Hey are you bringing my work over this afternoon?
Bren: Yeah, I was just getting it all together for you
Me: Oh joy, things I have to look forward to.
Me: I seriously don't know what is wrong with me!
Bren: I will be over in about 45
Me: okay see you then

While I wait for her to arrive, I grab a cold washcloth and put it on my forehead and close my eyes. *Is this ever going to stop?* Of course, right when I'm about to drift off, Bren arrives on the scene. She has all my books and assignments, and she even brought me a joint.

"I hear this is supposed to help with the nausea," she says as she winks at me.

"Good thinking!" I reply. "Let's go on the back porch."

We head out to the back porch and get settled in. I pull my feet up beneath me and grab a lighter.

"So, how has school been?"

"Not nearly as great without you there."

"I hope to go back on Monday, but this feeling won't go away. I seriously don't know what is going on."

As I pass the joint in her direction, she looks at me and asks, "Silly question, but could you be pregnant?"

Shocked, I reply, "What? *No*. Shit, could I be?"

Bren looks at me and says, "When did you have your last period? I had mine the week before prom, and we are usually not that far apart."

I pull out my phone and check the calendar; I haven't had a period in almost seven weeks.

Oh, Jesus. This can't be real. Looking at my calendar, I start repeating, "No, no, no, no, *no*. It can't be. *No*."

A lone tear falls down my cheek; I quickly wipe it away and look up at Bren.

"Oh, girl, we need to run out and get you a test. No matter what, I am here for you. But, first things first. Finish this joint with me before we find out if you can't anymore." Bren was serious, so we did, then she made me get into her car and drive to the store for a test. She is with me every step of the way. Where has this version of my friend Bren been? I am like dead weight walking; she has to push me along. Quickly, we buy the test and go straight back to my house. *I can do this; it is just a little test; it won't change my life or anything. Yeah right.*

I walk out of the bathroom with the test on the sink still and sit down next to Bren.

"What did it say?"

"We have to wait a few more minutes then go and check." I feel numb all over. *This can't be happening. My mom is going to kill me. My life is over.*

As the minutes go by, I sit there with so many thoughts in my head. When the time is up, I make my way to the bathroom with Bren on my heels.

I look down at the test and start to cry—two pink lines. *I'm pregnant.* Bren looks over my shoulder to see the test.

"Shit, girl! Who did you sleep with?" Bren exclaims, and then she looks at me. I am nothing but a crying mess, so with her arms wrapped around me, we sink to the floor.

"It was one stupid night. I don't want to talk about it." Again, I keep that night to myself. Eventually it will have to come out.

♡

James

I can't get the hug out of my head from that night. She felt so good in my arms. But now I don't know where she is or if she is okay. It's been over two weeks since I saw Kat walk through her door. She's never been gone off the grid for this long before. I wish I could ask Jayce about her, see if he knows anything, but then he would start to ask questions. What I really want to do is punch him in the face for treating her the way he did on prom night. I am just glad she felt like my cafe was a safe place, and even better, the fact that she trusted me to take her home.

This girl doesn't even know she has me wrapped around her finger. Hell, I want to protect her like she is mine. I want to make her mine in more ways than one, but I can't. I know her eighteenth birthday is coming up, but I don't know the date, and she has graduation too. These things should be enough to halt my thoughts about her, but there is just something that draws me to her. It may be her innocence, but she is so beautiful.

I hope she's okay, because it is killing me, not knowing.

Chapter Eight

Katarina

I don't know how long we sat on the bathroom floor, Bren holding me and rubbing my back as I cried, but eventually she had to leave—telling me to call her whenever I needed her—and I crawled into bed to sleep.

My mom has been home from work for a while now; I have been avoiding her since she got home. I decide to go into my bathroom and splash some cold water on my face to see if that would make me feel any better. Unfortunately, it won't wash away the fact that I'm pregnant.

"K, dinner's ready, are you coming down?" yells Mom up to me.

I crack my door and yell back. "I'll be there in a minute, Mom."

I drag myself out my room and down the stairs, plastering on a happy face.

"K, you okay? You still don't look great," my mom says to me as I take a seat at the table. She made teriyaki chicken and rice, and it smelled good for the first second but now suddenly, it makes me sick to my stomach.

"Yeah, Mom. I still don't feel great, but I'll be okay. This looks great," I lie. I pick my fork up and stab a piece of chicken, forcing myself to put it in my mouth and eat it. *Okay, one piece down, so many more to go. I* continue to eat and hold my sick feeling at bay. When dinner is done, I help clean up some before I head back to my room.

My mom is going to kill me when she finds out I'm pregnant.

I don't know what to do, blurt out I was raped and I'm pregnant? I'm not sure I can even say the words out loud. Whenever I think about it, my heart races and I feel like I'm going to faint. I still have to figure out what I want to do about this pregnancy. I could have an abortion, I know. And that would be the safest option. But this baby feels very real to me already, and I'm not sure I can do that. Should I keep it? Or give it up for adoption? I feel so lost right now.

One week until my mom's wedding.

Two weeks until graduation.

Three weeks until my birthday.

I'll wait until after my birthday to tell her; then I will be an adult and she can't dictate what I should do. I still don't know if I'll tell her about the rape. Maybe it's time to think about talking to someone about what happened to me.

Monday comes around, and back to school I go. Thankfully, my school was smart and had finals the week before prom and any make-ups the week after prom. Classes are done, and fun is to be had this last week. Only problem is, I am sick all the time and have no energy. All I want to do is sleep the days away.

Bren meets me every morning, and the first thing out of her mouth is always, "How are you doing?"

And every morning I lie and say, "Great!"

She knows I'm being a sarcastic brat, but she doesn't pry.

After school on Wednesday, I decide I am ready to go downtown again, to face the people I have been avoiding and have some fun, get outside and be a little bit normal again.

**Me: Hey I'm going to go to Bren's house after school; she will
give me a ride home later.**
Mom: Okay, don't be home too late
Me: Sure mom no later than 10
Mom: Sounds good
Me: Love you Mom
Mom: Love you too

"All set for after school, Bren, I just have to be home no later
than ten."

Bren, a bit surprised with what I just said, replies, laughing,
"Since when is your mom okay with you being out until ten at
night?"

"I know, right? I figured I was going to get a hard time from her."

School finishes up for the day, and Bren and I head to her car.
She looks at me with a cigarette in her hand. "You mind?"

"Your car, go for it, and hand one to me," I reply

"Um, are you sure? You shouldn't be smoking, K," Bren says

"With the crap I have been going through, one won't kill me, or
this—" I point to my stomach.

"If you say so," she says, "but only one."

I love this girl and her concern; I just hope she doesn't become
the overbearing mother figure I can see her becoming with me. She
has done a complete one-eighty on me—first it was all about the
party and having fun, and now it's all about being the best friend I
could ever ask for and concerned all the time.

♡♡

James

Today I decide to stop hiding out in The Java and get back into my
routine of heading up to the park in the afternoons. Today seems as

if it is my lucky day, because Kat is here with her friend Bren. Something is wrong—or maybe just different—with her, though. She looks pale and tired. I have to hold myself back from running to her side and asking if she is okay. She starts making the rounds with all the people hanging out and then looks up; she sees me and smiles then goes back to her socializing.

That smile just about kills me—it pierces my heart. But with that smile, I notice it doesn't reach her eyes. Finally, she makes her way over to where I am.

"Hey, James," she says. "Thanks again for the ride home the other night."

"*Wait*. He's the one that gave you a ride home? How did this happen?" Bren asks with narrowed eyes.

Kat looks over to Bren and says, "I walked to The Java right before it closed. James offered me a ride home."

"I was a perfect gentleman, just providing a ride." I hold my hands up in surrender because this girl looks like she is about ready to pounce.

I look over to Kat and notice a bit of her smile has fallen. *What just happened? What did I do or say?* It was almost as if I disappointed her with my response, like she was expecting me to declare something between us. I so would declare she was mine if I could, but not yet; I can't do that just yet.

"So, ladies, what are you up to this beautiful day?" I ask.

"I haven't been down here in a while, so I figured I would stop in before I had no way to get here anymore. with graduation in two weeks. I won't have a car to get around, so unless Miss Bren over here wants to drive all over the place to grab me, I'll be stuck at home, waiting for my birthday to arrive and praying I get a car. Though, I think that is wishful thinking," Kat says.

"You won't be stuck in that house of yours, don't you worry your pretty little head," Bren says, patting her on the head. "Plus, we have your mom's wedding, your eighteenth birthday, and Grad Night to think about."

I laugh and say, "Looks like you all have a lot to celebrate the next two weeks. Make sure you stop into The Java on your birthday, and I'll treat you both to a drink."

God, I want to stay here all day and talk to her. She still doesn't look great, like she has been sick and isn't quite over it yet. Despite all that, she still looks beautiful.

"Well, ladies, I have to get back to The Java. Don't be a stranger. Have a great afternoon."

I turn and walk away. Glancing back over my shoulder, I notice Kat is watching me retreat down the street. Looks like I only have to wait another two weeks to see if she likes me the way I hope she does.

Chapter Nine

WEDDING DAY

Katarina

Here it is, the day that I have been dreading—my mother's wedding day. One good thing about this day is that I get to go get pampered at the salon, even though it will be with my mom. We get our nails done while getting pedicures then move over to get our hair blown out and styled for the wedding. My mother forgoes a veil, thank God, and goes for a delicate tiara piece, while I get flowers put into a pretty up-do with my curls hanging down around my face. Once we are done, we go back to our soon-to-be-vacated home and get dressed. Bren is waiting for us when we get there. I may feel beautiful today, but I also feel sick to my stomach.

I am so grateful to have Bren here with me. Once we are done getting ready, we move toward my mom's car and head to the church. So many people have already arrived; we park in the back and slip inside. Bren leaves us in the bridal room to take her place on a pew. I slap a smile on my face and go over to my mom.

"You look beautiful today, Mom. I may not seem like it, but I am happy for you." She wraps her arms around me and gives me a tight squeeze. "Are you ready?"

"More than you know, sweetie," she says. We walk out to the huge doors leading into the church, and as the doors open, I walk my mom down the aisle. The look on my step-dad-to-be's face is one of pure delight. I hand my mom over to him and take my spot to the left of her.

The ceremony is short; they have both done this before. As I stand there and watch them, I think to myself that this will never happen for me. No one will want a girl who has a baby. No one will love me once they know. No one will want me. I brush off my thoughts, and as I do, the ceremony is wrapping up. I hear, "You may now kiss the bride" and then everyone starts clapping. I may not be happy about this, but I will do what I have to for my mom.

The reception is at a small venue near the Old Port; I catch a ride with Bren, my support system for the day. We dance and eat dinner and go through all of the normal wedding traditions. When it is time for my mom to go, she comes over to me and Bren and gives us both a big hug.

She whispers in my ear, "Thank you for being here today. I love you. Don't burn down the house."

They get into the car and head off to Boston for the weekend while I'm stuck at home packing for the big move.

"Want me to stay?" Bren asks when we get back to my house that night.

"No, I just need to be alone tonight. I'm tired and am going to go to sleep."

This day sucked, and I want nothing more than for it to be over.

Chapter Ten

GRADUATION DAY

Katarina

I can't believe it is almost over—one walk across the stage, and I will have finally graduated. The problem is, I am still pregnant, and still have no direction. College was the plan—but now I don't see it as an option at all.

Arriving at the auditorium, I wave goodbye to my mom as she heads to her seat with my new stepdad. He's slowly—very slowly—growing on me. I know he loves my mom and wants what's best for her and me both. Truth is, he doesn't know me, and this pregnancy isn't going to endear me to him.

"I can't believe this day has arrived! We are almost outta here!" Bren says as I walk up to her. She gives me a huge hug. "How are you feeling?"

"I actually feel pretty good today; I think this sickness may be finally going away," I answer honestly for the first time in weeks.

"Great. Are you excited for this weekend? I have it all planned out. My parents actually agreed to have a joint graduation and birthday party for you! Saturday can't come soon enough." Bren jumps up and down on the balls of her feet as she tells me; I think she is more excited than I am.

Before we know it, Sister Theresa is telling us to line up. "Here we go!"

We all line up, and on our cue, we walk into the auditorium, where the crowd of parents and friends goes crazy; flashes pulse over and over from cameras, and the hooting and hollering can be heard from miles away—you could feel the excitement in the room.

Sitting there in the auditorium, waiting to hear my name be called, is surreal. I am graduating high school, and in a week's time I will be an adult.

As I sit there waiting for my name to be called, I twist my fingers. This is an exciting day, but also a day where a new life for me will start, and I have no idea where that life will lead me. I'm scared, but I don't know who to tell or what to say to them. I'm ashamed of my recent actions that lead me to the place I find myself today— a knocked-up teenager. One week and I am going to be eighteen; one week, and I am going to tell my mom I am pregnant. I don't know why I feel it's so important to wait until I'm eighteen to tell her, but that's what I've planned and I don't know what else to do.

As I sit waiting for my turn to walk across the stage and take possession of my diploma, I start thinking about how I have no proof that I was raped. Why didn't I report it? Why was I even there to begin with? I put myself in a terrible position and I've paid the price. I messed up, I shouldn't have done the drugs and been drinking. This would have never happened if I had left that stuff alone. I feel so stupid. Will Bren hate me for not confiding in her? Will my mom hate me? I can't stop all the questions that keep invading my mind. After the questions, I start thinking about the guy. If I tell people what happened, will he come after me? What if he finds out I'm pregnant? I've seen those stories about rapists getting custody of their kids. I want nothing to do with him ever again. The thought of having to see him for the rest of my life makes me sick at my stomach. I'm lost in a tornado of questions while my classmates joyfully accept their diplomas, looking forward to their future.

I am so deep in thought I don't even realize my line has moved until Grace, who is sitting next to me, taps me on the shoulder.

"Let's go, Kat, it's our turn!" she says, knocking me out of my thoughts.

When my name is finally called, I stride across the stage and accept my diploma from Sister Theresa while simultaneously shaking her outstretched hand. "Congratulations, Katarina."

"Thanks," I reply.

As I continue to walk, I hear Bren yelling out, "Go, Kat!" and my mom's voice rises above the crowd, calling "That's my girl! I love you, Kat!"

This is it, the final name is called, and our valedictorian ends her speech with a loud, *"We did it! We graduated!"*

She and the rest of the graduating class switched their tassels from one side to the other, but that was a moot point since soon the entire class tossed their caps into the air with a loud burst of noise and laughter.

Once I find my cap, I go searching for my best friend. She spots me and comes barreling at me with her arms wide open. The next thing I know, we are tumbling to the ground; I can't control my laughter, but the look on Bren's face is much different.

"Oh, my God, are you okay? I didn't hurt you, did I?"

It takes me a second to realize why she is so concerned, and I love her for that, but one stumble to the ground won't hurt anything.

"I'm fine, don't worry so much," I whisper.

We get up off the ground and notice that our parents are there laughing at us.

"They act like they're glad to get out of this place," Bren's dad says with a chuckle.

Everyone joins in our laughter.

The next thirty minutes consists of a photo shoot right outside the doors of the school in front of the school's sign. My face is starting to hurt from all the smiling. *Ugh, parents.*

Finally, when they have what they decide is enough pictures in various combinations, we head away from the school. We all have plans to go out to lunch together to celebrate, and they chose a place right downtown in the Old Port. Lucky me. This is definitely not the place I want to be today with my mom; I don't want her to realize how much time I spend here.

We find parking in the parking garage and head down the street near the park and straight past The Java. As we walk by, I steal a quick glance inside and notice James staring at me. His stare is so intense. I smile at him as we walk by and head to the restaurant by the water.

Lunch is nice and relaxing, and I am actually able to eat something and not want to throw up for once. Then, the questions start to flow from both sides of parents. *What are your plans for the summer? "What are your plans for the fall?" Bren's parents ask me and mine ask her at the same time. We both start to laugh as we look at each other like a pair of deer in headlights.* We have no answers, especially me, so we direct the conversation to the celebration next week.

I look to Bren's parents and say, "Thank you for allowing me to celebrate my birthday at the graduation party."

"You're welcome, Kat. We look forward to celebrating your birthday. Eighteen, right?" Bren's dad asks.

"Yes, I'll be eighteen. My birthday is actually on Saturday, so it is great timing."

My mom looks at me with surprise on her face. *Shit! I forgot to tell her about the party on Saturday.*

"Mom, Bren's parents are having a graduation party for us on Saturday, and because my birthday is the same day, we are going to celebrate with all our friends. Of course you're invited. I'm sorry, I forgot to tell you about it."

"Sweetie, it's okay, I know you have been busy and not feeling well, but we will be there. We can celebrate your birthday as a family on Friday. Go to dinner, maybe?"

"Can we make it an early dinner, Mom? I was going to spend Friday night with Bren so that I am there to help with the party Saturday morning."

"Sure, that's fine."

We finish up lunch, and thankfully, Bren drove here separately from her mom and dad, so we are able to escape the parents and head in our own direction. We both turn and wave to our parents as we thank them for lunch and say bye. We end up going right past The Java again and decide to stop in.

James

I wasn't expecting to see her today; she was surrounded by parents and Bren as she walked right by my place. I couldn't help but stare at her as she walked by. I almost thought she wasn't going to look in my direction, but then she did, and a genuine smile crossed her face. I nodded my head in recognition as she continued to walk down the street.

I honestly wanted to rush out that door and pick her up and kiss her. I knew today was graduation day, and that meant I was one step and one week closer to being able to tell her how I feel about her. We have such an age gap, my twenty-two to her eighteen. It's not so much the years as it is the place we've been in life, too. I don't know how I will tell her I want her, that I am falling for her, or even if I will have the guts to tell her, but to know that I can soon makes me so happy.

I snap out of my thoughts and go back to work. Jayce just walked in the door, so it is my time to head to the office once he gets behind the counter. About an hour goes by and I hear Jayce holler, "Graduates in the house, everyone!"

Hope flares within me, and I exit my office and there she is, standing there looking a bit tense at the counter, talking to Jayce with Bren at her side. I stand off to the side just watching her, and as if she can feel my eyes on her, she looks in my direction, so I smile at her, push myself off the wall, and walk over to them.

"What's this I hear about a graduation?" I ask.

"That would be us, one step closer to absolute freedom," Bren answers.

"Well, since congratulations are in order, your coffee is on me." I notice that Kat hasn't said anything, so I look directly at her and say, "Congrats, Kat."

"Thank you," she replies shyly.

Jayce interrupts our mutual staredown with a, "What will it be?"

He did that on purpose. I get it, he likes her, but she has made it clear that she just wants to be friends. I hope one day he realizes he has no chance with her. Hell, I just hope I have a chance. I look over to Kat again, and she has a completely different look on her face, almost as if something has spooked her outside. I follow her line of sight and see a guy across the street who appears to be staring straight at her. Kat looks like she saw a ghost, and as I examine her more closely, she seems to be shaking. *Why would she fear anyone, especially someone who is across the street and nowhere near her?*

I walk up next to her and lightly tap her arm just enough to get her attention. "Kat, hey, are you okay? You look like you just saw a ghost."

Kat quickly snaps out of it and looks right at me. She still has a slight tremble to her body, but she nods and flashes a brief smile. "Yeah, I'm fine, I just spaced out. I've been so tired lately."

I don't believe a word she said; something is wrong, and I have a bad feeling about that guy across the street. One way or another, I will find out what this is about.

From that point on, Kat acts just fine, like nothing happened. The girls grab their coffees from Jayce and go sit at one of the tables. I take this as my cue to head back to the office and finish my work. Before I head back, I turn to the girls and say, "Congrats again, ladies. Enjoy the coffee."

I turn toward the office and decide to make it my mission to figure out what's going on with Kat. But not today.

Chapter Eleven

Katarina

No, not again. Why is he there, and why is he just staring at me? He is the one that hurt me, not the other way around. What does he want from me? I can't let him find out about the baby.

This guy, he scares me; I wish he would just go away. I can't tell anyone about him because then they will figure out what happened to me. It isn't until James is by my side, tapping my shoulder, that I'm knocked back into reality and realize I'm shaking.

Once we're settled at the table with our drinks, Bren eyes me. "So what was that about?"

"What was what about?" I reply.

With a frustrated look on her face, Bren motions her head to the back of The Java where the office sits. "Him, you, the whispering off to the side?"

"It was nothing. He just was asking if I was feeling better."

She looked at me like she didn't believe me. *What is it with people today not believing a word out of my mouth?* I suppose they have a reason to act that way, given how much I'm not telling anyone, but still.

"Moving on. So, what kind of cake do you want at the party?" Bren asks.

"Let's go with chocolate cake with strawberry frosting; it's my favorite."

"Sounds good to me. We'll actually have two cakes: one is for the grad party, and the other is your birthday cake. This is going to be so much fun! We just have to deal with the parents until cake time, and after that, my parents have agreed to take off for a while, so we will have until midnight to party," Bren says.

"I really can't wait, Bren. This is going to be so much fun, and at least I get to have some fun before I tell my mom what is going on with me. I plan on telling her on Sunday after I get home," I confess in a hushed voice so no one can hear me.

"Do you want me there? I will be if you need me."

"As much as I love you, I need to do this just me and Mom. Thank you for being there for me when I need you."

"Definitely, no problem, I'll always be there."

We finish off our coffee and decide to head out, and as we walk to the door, we both turn around and wave goodbye to Jayce. He is a good guy, but not the guy for me. In fact, I don't know if there *is* a guy for me anymore.

Sunday night, Bren stays at my house, because I needed a ride Monday to a doctor's appointment—my first doctor's appointment since I found out I was pregnant. Well, it is really just an appointment to confirm what we already know. I've waited long enough.

Monday morning comes, and we head off to Planned Parenthood, since I'm doing this without my mom's knowledge. The ride to the office is quiet; I'm not in the mood to talk. Heck, I still don't even know what I'm going to do. So, we will see what happens once we get there. I think it is all the fear of the unknown. I should have just told my mom from the start.

The ride is too short, and before I know it, we are ringing the buzzer to be let into the building. Once we get up to the counter and check in, I have a stack of paperwork to fill out.

When I've finished, and expertly skipped over the insurance information since it will come right back to my mom, I turn in my papers and take a seat next to Bren. She doesn't talk, and that's fine by me because I'm stuck in my head, overthinking everything.

"Katarina?" a woman asks from a door that was closed moments ago.

Standing, I silently walk with her, Bren trailing behind me. The woman instructs me to leave a urine sample in the bathroom, and when I'm finished with that, she leads us to an exam room, where she asks me to undress and put on a paper gown.

When I'm decent, the doctor comes into the exam room with a small computer and asks me some basic health questions. Then the hard questions start.

"How many partners have you had?" she asks matter of factly.

"I've had one."

"Was this someone you know and trust?"

Dipping my head, not really wanting to talk about this I answer, "Not exactly. We had met that night and now I'm here because I think I'm pregnant."

"Kat, I have to recommend that we do a series of STD testing. This way we can be certain that you have a clean bill of health. We can take some blood and when we do the exam, I'll just do a quick swab and send everything to the lab. How does that sound?" Fear tears through me at the thought that the guy may have given me more than a baby.

"Kat, I think it's a good idea. I know it's a scary thought but, it's better to know you're healthy than wonder," Bren urges.

"Okay, I'll do it." I blurt it out with all the confidence in the world, even though the thought of having an STD kills me inside.

The doctor continues asking her questions about my health as the reality of my life takes over my thoughts.

"When did you last have your period?" she asks, never looking up from her computer.

"March thirtieth," I tell her softly.

"Well, you are indeed pregnant, and by my calculations, you are about nine weeks along, with a due date of December twentieth." Finally, she looks up at me, with a smile on her face. It quickly falls when she sees me. "Is everything okay?"

Bren looks at me and says, "Hey, Kat, what's going on? Are you second guessing yourself and your decision to keep the baby?"

I don't answer either one of them immediately. I feel paralyzed in the reality of these monumental decisions.

"Bren, I don't know if I can do this. We just graduated high school; college is where we are supposed to be in the fall. I just don't know what I want right now, except to wish that this never happened to begin with."

I look at Bren and see shock on her face. She looks at me like I am a stranger. I don't know what she wants me to do or say...I just don't know anymore.

The doctor looks at me with sympathy in her eyes and lets me know that we can go over the different options available to me, including abortion, and she encourages me to think through the options and the long term consequences of them. *Do I want to do this? Can I live with myself if I have an abortion?* As I sit there listening to the doctor, she lets me know that they can help me in whatever decision

I make, and if I choose to keep the baby they will help me with the process to get Medicaid so I will have medical coverage for me and the baby, before and after it is born.

With my options in mind, we walk out the door. Only a small moment passes before Bren's hand is on my arm, turning me around to face her. "What was all that about? You don't know what you are going to do? I thought you knew what you were going to do, and you knew you were going to welcome your child into the world?"

I wasn't expecting this from Bren; I figured she would understand that I needed time to think and figure it out. It is a lot to take on. I guess I was wrong, instead she stands there with judgment in her eyes and I'm chilled to realize that if my choice is abortion, she very likely won't be on my side.

We ride silently back to my house, and Bren dropped me off after giving me some vague excuse that she had things to do and couldn't stay. I knew she was pissed at me, and I understood, so I let her go, went to my room, and curled up on the bed. *What am I going to do? What should I do?*

Before I know it, my mom is walking into my room, and the light from the sun is low in the window. Apparently, the stress of the day took its toll on me, and I slept for several hours.

"You hungry?" Mom asks.

"I can eat," I tell her.

"Let's order a pizza tonight; I'm too tired to cook."

"Sounds good to me."

Mom leaves my room, and I peel myself out of bed. While washing my face to wake myself up a bit, I hear the doorbell ring. *That can't be the pizza already.*

"Kat, someone is here to see you," Mom calls.

Walking toward the front door, I see Bren standing on the other side with an apologetic look on her face.

"Can I come in? I need to talk to you."

"Sure." I agree and yell into the kitchen, "We will be in my room."

"Okay," Mom yells back.

Bren and I walk to my room in silence. *God, this silence stuff lately between us is starting to kill me.*

After I close the door, Bren wastes no time. "I'm so sorry. I can't even imagine what you're going through and how hard of a decision any and all of this is to make. I am so sorry."

I wrap my arms around her and hug her. "It's okay. I wish it was easy, but it isn't."

"I know, and I'm sorry for not seeing it from your point of view. I was just so excited with the thought of being an auntie."

"Bren—"Just then, the doorbell rings, signaling the pizza's arrival. With a smile, I dismiss the temptation to confess all and instead ask, "Want some pizza?"

She smiles. "Sure."

This time, the silence between us doesn't bother me, because I know that no matter what, Bren will always be there for me.

$\heartsuit$

James

Once again, Kat seems to have disappeared this week. I've been worried about her since her graduation night, and I wish I knew what was going on. The fear I saw in her eyes killed me to see. I wanted to take her in my arms and promise her that everything will be okay. When I first saw her, she had such a sweet, innocent look in her eyes. Something has dimmed her light, and I want to fix it.

Jayce has been on my case lately, asking me what is wrong. Apparently, I have been a bear to work for. It's all because of Kat.

I hope she comes by on Saturday. It's her birthday, she will finally be eighteen, and I can kiss her without feeling like a creep. I can tell her I want her, and after all these months, find out if she feels the same.

Then maybe I will have the chance to put the light back in her eyes.

Two days, but it will feel like two years.

Chapter Twelve

Katarina

My birthday is tomorrow. I checked the mail today, and in it was a card for me from my father, who hasn't called or even made an attempt to see me. I tear it open to see a graduation card. *Did he even remember my birthday?* In the card is a check for one thousand five hundred dollars and just his signature scrawled on the cheap card.

What am I going to do with the money? I briefly think about buying a car, but I still don't have my license, and then I think about calling Bren and having a fun night out and shopping, but reality quickly intrudes—I am going to need this money for my baby.

I think I just made my decision to keep the little one growing in my tummy. Just as I make my decision, my phone rings, and caller ID shows Planned Parenthood. I reluctantly answer the call with a timid, "Hello."

"Hi, I'm looking for Katarina, is she available?"

"This is her. How can I help you?"

"I was calling to let you know we have your test results back.

Usually we would call you into the office, but I have great news and I didn't want you to have to wait! Everything came back clear."

"Thank God." I let out the breath I was holding.

"I hope you have a great day, bye!" The perky tech ends the call before I can even say good-bye back.

My mom comes home a while later, and I have already put the check into my bank account through that little app thing on my phone. Today I decided I was going to find an apartment of my own. Mom isn't very happy with me; she says that money is supposed to go toward my school in the fall, and it isn't to blow on unnecessary things.

"It's my money, and I can do whatever I want with it. I'm going to get an apartment and a job. I'm not going to college."

"You are going to do what?" she cried, eyes wide. "Why aren't you going to college? What are you talking about, Kat? Don't do this. You're going to throw your life away."

"If I can have a baby, I think I can decide what to do with my money. I put it into savings, and I am getting an apartment."

"I can't believe you—Wait, what? *You're pregnant?*" As the weight of my words settles around us, she begins to cry.

Shit, what did I just do?

"Yes, Mom, I'm pregnant. Almost ten weeks along now."

"I can't believe this. Fine, you want to make adult decisions? Then make them on your own. I knew you've been sneaking out and lying and God knows what, with that girl Bren. You are *done* here. Tomorrow, you are on your own, and don't come crying back to me." Her anger is getting the best of her in this moment, but the stab to the heart is just as painful.

So much for celebrating my birthday tonight. Wheeling around, I go to my room and start to pack a bag. Most of my stuff is already packed anyway for the move to Kyle's, which is apparently now nothing I need to be worried about. Tears run down my face, and at this point, I know I have to prove myself to her. I am going to keep this baby, even if it kills me in the process. I didn't think she would go straight to kicking me out, but whatever. She's obviously not interested in anything I have to say. And frankly, that's nothing new.

While I'm packing my bag, I call Bren.

"Hello?" she answers.

"Bren, it's me. I-I-I need a place to stay," I stammer.

"Are you okay? What happened? Of course you can stay here, you were going to anyway," my best friend rambles.

"Can you come get me?"

"I'm leaving my house now; I'll be there soon."

I finish packing then go out to the front porch to wait for Bren. Tears continue to stream down my face and drip onto my pants.

I look up and see my mom through the window, standing in the living room with tears streaming down her face. Kyle is by her side, with his arm wrapped around her in comfort. Seems like everyone has someone but me. But now I have someone who needs me, and I will show them that I can be exactly what this baby needs.

"Sweetie, what happened?" Bren asks the second I'm settled into her passenger seat.

I manage to sob out, "I accidentally told her I was pregnant when we were arguing about college, and she told me to get out and not come back."

"She said what? What a *bitch*." I can hear the anger in her voice. "You can stay here for a while, sweetie. Maybe she will cool off." She lets me cry while she drives, and once we're at her house, she pulls up in the drive but doesn't move to get out.

"What am I going to do? She got pissed that I said I was using the money my dad sent me to get an apartment, and said I was throwing my life away by not going to college in the fall, and then it just came out of my mouth. I'm so stupid," I bellow.

"You are *not* stupid. Don't say that."

Bren gathers me into her arms, letting me cry on her shoulder for a few moments before she tells me she's hungry and surely the baby needs to eat. We go inside, and while I head into Bren's bedroom, she splits off to the kitchen. I don't know if I will be able to eat, but she brings me a sandwich anyway. After just a few bites, I crawl up on her pillow and pass out.

When the sun streams through the windows, it takes me a minute to remember where I am and why. Gently, in an effort not to wake Bren, who is curled up beside me, I move into the bathroom.

Before I can close the door, a sleepy Bren mumbles, "Happy birthday, Kat."

Oh, yeah. "Thanks. What a happy birthday it is too," I say sarcastically

"We will make it great, Kat. You're eighteen now, and you have your whole adult life ahead of you, and we have a party to throw today!"

I brighten up a bit at the prospect of a fun day and a party. When I'm finished in the bathroom, I come back to see Bren is dressed and applying her makeup.

"Hurry and get dressed; we have lots to do today. First stop is The Java for coffee and breakfast."

The prospect of seeing James puts pep in my step, and I grab some clothes. Once dressed, I put on some mascara and some pink lip gloss.

"Ready," I tell her.

"Let's go."

James

I woke up this morning with a plan—I am going to kiss that girl today. With a purpose, I walked downstairs to The Java and started getting everything ready to open. Once my second morning worker comes in, I head to my office to do paperwork.

When, I wander out a while later to ask about a missing time sheet, I am surprised and pleased to see both Kat and Bren are at the counter ordering coffee and pastries.

"Well, look who it is. You're here early today, aren't you?" I say with a grin as I walk toward them. "Cammie, their stuff is on the house today. I hear it's someone's eighteenth birthday!" I give her a hug, wish her happy birthday, and give her a small kiss on the cheek before pulling back to see her beautiful face turning pink with embarrassment.

"Thanks, you really didn't have to do that. Bren was buying."

I chuckle. "Well, I did promise to buy you a coffee on your birthday, so no worries. How are you doing today, birthday girl?"

"I'm good, excited for this afternoon and tonight; we are having a party at Bren's house. You should stop by tonight," she says, and then the most comical shocked look flashes on her face. I think she surprised herself, and it's all I can do not to kiss her right now.

"I'll try. Bren, can you write your address down so I have it?" I ask.

Bren nods and digs in her purse for a piece of paper and a pen.

I wasn't ready for her arrival this early in the day; I was hoping she would stop in later today or tonight. Pulling her a little bit away from the counter, I ask, "Are you okay? You look like you have been crying, and no one should be crying on their birthday." I rub my thumbs under her puffy eyes.

She pulls her face away and says, "I'm fine, thanks for asking."

I want to kiss her. Her eyes look so sad, even though she is trying to act happy. I let her pull away with a smile and a wave. She walks back over to the counter where Bren is just grabbing their coffee and pastries. They grab a table, and I make myself busy so I can lurk near the front and watch. I wish I could figure out what is going on in that pretty little head of hers. Until then, I will give her the space she wants and see her tonight.

When Bren notices I am getting ready to walk away, she calls me over. "James, here is my address; the party starts early because we are having a graduation BBQ, but you're welcome to stop by at any time. Party ends at midnight. See you later." Kat is looking right at me the entire time, like she wants to look into my soul.

She has me, and she doesn't even know it yet.

Chapter Thirteen

Katarina

Why does he care about me or why I was crying? He has never even hinted at being interested in me, not like today. He kissed me, albeit on the cheek, but he still kissed me and wrapped me in his arms for a hug. The way he looked at me when he slid his thumbs under my eyes... it was different than before. Unless I am going crazy. Which is possible at this point.

Once we finish breakfast, we head out. It's nine-thirty in the morning, and we have a lot to do today, so we head back to Bren's house. When we arrive, her parents are in the kitchen drinking coffee.

"Hey, girls, where have you been?" Bren's mom, Tina, asks.

"I took Kat to The Java for breakfast for her birthday, though I got out of paying because the owner has the hots for Kat!" she answers back.

Mortified, I shoot Bren a look and squawk, "*What?* You have no clue what you are talking about. He is just a nice guy."

A look passes between Bren and her mom, and they both say in unison, "Riiiiight."

"You both are crazy," I say as I feel my face heat. "I'm going to go take a shower."

As I walk away, I hear Bren say to her mom, "I invited him over tonight for the party. I bet he shows up, that will prove I'm right." And then they both erupt into a fit of giggles.

When I get out of the shower, I lay out the clothes I want to wear this afternoon. I choose a cute, short blue dress with maroon accents and a light sweater to go with it. The days are warm, but the nights get chilly here in Maine, even in early summer. I don't want to get dressed for the party yet, so I toss on a pair of leggings and an oversized T-shirt and walk back out to the kitchen where they all still sit.

"So, what do we need to get done before the party today?" I ask as I approach.

"Really, we don't have to do a lot; we have an event planner coming over in about an hour with her crew to set up, and the caterer will be here soon after that," Bren's mom announces.

"Whoa, wait. You have an event planner for this party? Bren, why didn't you tell me? I wouldn't have agreed to celebrating my birthday tonight too." This is really out of my comfort zone. I feel like the poor relation. With my mom raising my brother and I on her own after dad left early on, she does her best. We've managed all these years with her working full time as an insurance adjuster. Dad pays for my tuition and school uniforms, and he sends just enough but never enough for any luxury items.

"Yes, Kat, we have it all planned out. It was nothing to add a cake and to sing 'Happy Birthday.' You are my best friend; of course I want to celebrate with you," Bren argues.

Tina comes over and gives me a hug. "Sweetie, really, this is not a big deal. We seriously just added a cake to the plans for later in the night. Bren wanted to help you celebrate, and we are more than happy to do it."

"Thank you, all of you. It—it means a lot. So, Bren, what do we have to do then? You said we had a lot to do today."

"Well, seeing as it is your birthday, I am taking you to get your nails done and then your hair; we need to make you look *hot* tonight, especially since James will be here." She winks at me.

"Oh, Bren, no. You've done so much already. There is no need to do that. And who knows if James will even show up—*not that it matters.*" I pin her with a stare but she ignores me totally.

"My turn for a shower and then we're off, Kat, no argument," Bren shouts as she walks away, leaving me in the kitchen with her parents.

"Thank you both again, you are way too kind to me. I really don't need a big deal made for my birthday. This is Bren's graduation party," I say as I sit down at the island.

"Really, Kat, Bren is the happiest she's been in her life since she met you. You are more like a sister to her, so don't worry about it. As long as you are both happy today, we are happy," her dad says to me as he sips his coffee sitting next to me.

Once Bren graces us with her presence again, we head for the door and to her car. Before I know it, we are in front of this small, upscale salon, and once again, I feel like it is too much. What kind of life did I live before I met Bren? She may be a bit crazy, but she sure is a great friend.

"I made my decision, Bren; I am going to keep the baby."

"Really? Oh my God, I get to be an auntie. I can't wait to buy tiny little clothes! What made you decide?"

"You, my mom…my stubbornness. My mom was so quick to assume that I was just a loser who got herself knocked up. She didn't have faith in my judgment for anything, much less consider what I might want to do. And you seemed to believe from the get-go that I could do it. I decided to believe you, not her, because lately it seems as if you are the only one that really knows me and cares about me."

"You're right, I do care about you, but I don't think I am the only one, Kat. I have no doubt your mom loves you; I think she's just afraid, given what happened with your brother. And James had a different look in his eye today when he watched you. Maybe today was the day he has been waiting for—maybe eighteen is the magic number, and he can actually show you he cares."

"I think you're crazy, Bren. We are barely friends. He gave me a ride home one night, and he didn't even try to flirt with me or kiss me."

"Kat, if you don't see it then I think you are the crazy one."

When she walks into the salon, I stand back with my jaw dropped. *I'm* crazy? I don't think so. He doesn't like me like that, and he sure as hell won't when he sees a growing belly. Doesn't matter how much I like him.

I have never been so spoiled. I was scrubbed, buffed, and even waxed—that was an interesting experience. My nails, fingers, and toes were done in a maroon color to match my dress accents. I decided it was time for a change, so I chopped my hair off—like, *a lot* of hair. I am now sporting a lob with some highlights, and I love it. I feel like a whole new person.

Back to the house, it's hard to believe it's the same place at all. Tables are scattered throughout the backyard, and a dance floor is laid with a canopy over the top of it, and when the lights go down, it will be lit with twinkle lights. I have never seen anything like what this place is turning into, and it is all for Bren and a little bit me.

Once I pick up my jaw off the ground, we go inside to get dressed for the afternoon and evening. Bren handles our makeup, and when we are happy with our reflections in the mirror, we make our way to the backyard, where people are starting to arrive. The DJ is starting up, and the food is starting to be passed around. This day has just flown by.

"Let's go," Bren says, and she proceeds to pull me into the center of the party. I don't recognize many people; I assume they are family friends of Bren. I do notice, however, that my mother and Kyle are missing from the scene. I don't know why I expected her to show up, but I guess I hoped just a little she would, even with what happened yesterday. It is my birthday, after all.

A couple hours later, when it starts to get dark out, our friends from school start to show up. The mood of the gathering has changed, and it is beginning to seem more like a party. Now the young outweigh the old. It is a barbecue, so even though it is catered, we have burgers and hotdogs, chicken and steak, and some amazing baked beans and potato salad, fruit salad, and everything you would want at something like this.

It's when I am sitting with Bren and a few of our friends that I notice my mom talking to Bren's parents like nothing even happened yesterday. I choose to ignore her and continue to have fun, though I do notice her take a look over in my direction. Kyle is right by her side, with a look on his face that says he isn't happy to be here.

Eventually, she walks over to me and pulls me off to the side. "I need to talk to you, Kat."

"I think you said enough yesterday when you kicked me out of the house." I try to pull out of her grip and walk away. "Mom, just leave me alone, I am not doing this today."

She won't let go, and I don't want to make a scene, so I stand there, glaring at her like the child I no longer want to be. "Fine. What the hell do you want?"

"We need to talk about yesterday, about what you told me, this plan you have with the money that was supposed to go toward your college. What on earth is going on with you lately?" she snarls at me.

"I'm not doing this here, Mom."

I yank my arm out of her grasp and walk away, but as I look up, I see half the party looking at us. So much for not making a scene. I wasn't paying any attention to where I was walking, and I end up bumping into someone nearby. Looking up, I find myself in the arms of the last person I ever want to see. Him touching me, with that ever-present smirk on his face, turns my knees to Jell-O. I end up on the ground, not knowing how I got there.

"Kat! Are you okay? What was that about?" Bren asks as she rushes over to me.

I shake myself out of the haze and ask, "What just happened?"

"You ran into Trent then you started pounding on his chest and screaming to let you go. He pushed you away, and you fell."

Trent. I now had a name instead of just a face. It didn't change the way I felt about him; he's a monster, he stole from me, and he has been watching me. Now I have his child inside me.

"I'm fine. Um, I'm just going to go inside for a bit."

"If you say so. I'll check on you in a bit," Bren says softly.

I walk toward the house, trying to keep the tears away until I get away from the party. I feel like an absolute fool. When I raise my eyes in the shadows, I see James staring at me, but I keep walking. I can't deal with this—it was an amazing day until my mom and the monster ruined it. I go straight for Bren's room and collapse on her bed, letting the tears fall.

I'm not alone long. I hear the door open slowly, and then I hear James's raspy voice. "Kat, are you okay?"

"Go away," I snap at him. I don't want him to see me like this. I'm humiliated enough between what happened with my mom and my apparent blackout with Trent. I want to be alone.

He cautiously approaches the side of the bed and sits down. "Kat, hey, what's going on?" he asks quietly as he moves my now-short hair away from my face and behind my ear. I didn't want to look at him, but I can't help it; his ice-blue eyes have a look of concern in them now, and I don't like that. Sitting up, I move out of his reach. His fingers brushing the side of my face felt good, but I can't let myself enjoy it—I am too messed up to deserve any kindness from him.

"I just had a fight with my mom. I'll be fine. Give me a few minutes, and I'll be all ready to party again," I reassure him. I don't think it worked, and I have no clue really why he cares. By now, I have stopped crying...well, I'm no longer sobbing—a few tears still manage to sneak down my face. I just need to get myself together and get back out there. I can't have James hearing about everything that is going on.

"Go on back outside. I need to clean up, and I will be back out there. I just needed a few minutes to pull myself together after the scene I caused."

James looks at me again with those eyes that could melt the panties off of anyone but are full of concern for me. Hesitantly, he stands up.

"Are you sure you are okay? You don't look like you are okay."

With a forced laugh, I say, "Yes, I am good. I promise."

"I can wait for you, walk out there together," he offers.

I still just want to be alone, so once again, I blow him off. He reluctantly walks out the door, looking back over his shoulder before he closes it. I let out a sigh of relief and go into Bren's bathroom to take a look at the damage I did to my face by bawling like a baby. This is bad, *really* bad; I don't think I can fix it on my own. Luckily, right then the door opens with my savior.

"Thank God it's you. I need you to fix this," I plead with her.

"I'm glad to see you are feeling a bit better, but before I fix this"—she waves her hand back and forth in front of my face— " you need to explain what happened tonight, and don't lie to me."

I let out a sigh and decide I can tell her a little something to appease her for now.

"That was one guy I do not want to see again, like ever. He can't know about the baby. I will do this on my own, with no help from him. It was and will stay one night that was a mistake."

It's like a light bulb goes off over her head, the way her eyes get wide with shock.

"Wait, you mean to tell me that Trent is the one who got you pregnant? This can't be, when... where... oh my God. I can't *believe* this!" Her voice has risen with every word and she's now shouting at me.

"Wait, why are you yelling at me? I don't understand. You were the one to bring me to that stupid party. The first one—that was, oh, let's say about ten weeks ago, actually about eleven weeks ago now. What did I do to piss you off?"

"Trent, h-h-he," she starts to sob. "He is the one I have been wanting to get with all year, but I could never catch his eye. I can't believe this. *You!* Fix your own damn face." She's raving with jealousy, but she doesn't even realize she has nothing to be jealous about.

Once again, a person I thought knew me and loved me has made assumptions without asking a single question about what happened. I am starting to think I never belonged in this world. I actually *know* I don't belong here, surrounded by her family and other friends, so instead of fixing my face and going back out to the party, I wash off every ounce of makeup, grab my purse and one duffel bag with enough for a few days, and leave out the front door.

Worst birthday *ever*.

James

When I walk around the house to the back where the party is, I stop in my tracks—Kat is on the ground with Bren by her side. I stand there watching her, and when she gets up and starts walking my way, she doesn't notice me at first because I am hidden in the shadows. As much as I want to go running over to her, I don't. When she does finally notice me, she has a look of shock on her face. Kat keeps walking into the house, and I stand there for a few minutes, trying to decide what to do. Unable to deny my pull toward her, I follow.

When I find her, she is sobbing on Bren's bed—it kills me to see her this way. After her telling me to go away multiple times, I finally listen and return to the party.

Something's not right here, and once again, I decide that I must figure it out. If I had shown up a bit earlier, I would have had a better clue as to what this was all about, so the only other way to get the scoop is to talk to Bren.

"Hey, Bren, what's going on with Kat? I saw her crying and run into the house," I ask when I approach her.

With a sigh, she gives me the rundown. "She had a fight with her mom but was okay after that, then in her hurry to walk away from her mom, she ran right into Trent's chest and just freaked out, started pounding on him and yelling for him to let go of her. Trent pushed her away, and she fell down. I really don't know what is going on with her. It was like she blacked out. She asked me what happened."

"Who is this Trent guy?" I ask with my jaw grinding in anger.

Bren points across the lawn to the guy, and the moment I see him, I recognize him as the guy who was watching Kat in my café that day from across the street. *What does he want with Kat?*

In a matter of seconds, I am right in front of him and ready for answers.

"What do you want with Kat?"

With a smirk on his face, he holds up his hands in denial. "I don't know what you're talking about. I was defending myself from her attack. She's a crazy bitch."

Without thinking, I grab him by his collar and pull him until we're nose to nose. "Stay away from her. I've seen you watch her, and I don't know what your deal is, but I will find out."

Bren comes storming out of the house as I walk away from Trent, but Kat is nowhere to be found. I continue to wait, but she never appears again. Twenty minutes later, I seek out Bren again and ask her if she has seen Kat.

"Nope," she says, popping the "p" before she turns back around, ignoring me. I decide to go check on her, but she's nowhere to be found. After rushing back outside to tell Bren—who bizarrely doesn't seem to care at all—I jog to my car.

I will find her, if it's the last thing I do.

Chapter Fourteen

Katarina

Now what do I do? I didn't think this far in advance, so here I am, walking down the street with my stuff, nowhere to go. Then I remember there's a park near the water not too far from here, so I head that direction. When I get there, I find a bench and take a seat, dropping my bag beside me. I have no missed calls or messages when I check my cell phone, which only confirms how alone I truly am.

The sky, dotted with stars, is peaceful. I get up and stand near the edge of the overlook, in a daze, looking out to sea. It's empty, like me. I feel like I am nothing—unwanted.

My mom is getting ready to go on her real honeymoon. They could only get away for the weekend right after the wedding before coming home to move into her husband's house.

My best friend is mad at me because I "slept" with the guy she likes. The guy who raped me.

I am pregnant by that guy, and alone, and everyone seems to

have someone but me. One step forward, and I would be falling toward the water and the rocks below. One step forward, and I wouldn't have to worry anymore. One step is all it would take.

I hear a car engine in the distance, getting closer. It occurs to me that Trent might be out looking for me after the scene I caused, or maybe it's the cops to tell me I can't be here. I lower myself down to sit on the edge and try to stay out of sight; I don't want to be found. But it didn't work.

I whip around when I hear James's voice behind me and start to lose my balance on the ledge. A moment ago, I wanted to walk off this ledge, because I was nothing to no one. But when my butt slips off and I start to fall, I panic and grab the edge in time. Suddenly, James is rushing over to me and grabbing my hands to pull me up. He holds me tightly in his arms once I'm back to standing, snapping, "What are you thinking, Kat? Are you okay?"

I sarcastically reply, "Just peachy."

"What are you doing here, and why the hell are you dangling over the edge?"

"James, you need to leave. You should go and leave me to this life I messed up all on my own before you get dragged down into it."

"Why did you leave the party at Bren's? Isn't that where you were staying tonight?"

"Yeah, well, not everything works out the way we want it to. I can't seem to find my place in this world, so I just came here to try to figure out what to do next."

Leaning forward, he lifts my chin with his finger so I will meet his eyes, and they're different than I've seen them before. Pity, sadness—I'm not sure what it is.

"I know someone who doesn't mind being around you—me. Come with me. I can't have you out here all night by yourself. A swim in those waters wouldn't be any fun, either. We can go to my place and talk. Tell me what's going on. I'm here for you, I want to be here for you."

I open my mouth to protest, but he simply wraps his arms around me for a tight hug and kisses my forehead.

"Come on," he says, grabbing my hand and leading us to his car.

"My bag!" I yelp, coming to a halt. He lets go long enough to grab the bag by the bench and comes immediately back to me. He puts my bag in the trunk and we both get into his gorgeous car. Once we get closer to Old Port, he drives to the back of The Java, parks, gets out of the car, then grabs my duffel out of the trunk and leads me inside the building, but through a different door than for his cafe. *He lives here?*

James is acting strange. I don't know what the change is, but I like it. He has never touched me like this. Maybe Bren was right. He doesn't know it, but tonight, he saved me, in more ways than one.

♡♡

James

"You want anything to drink, Kat?"

"No, thank you."

She's staring off into space, much like I found her tonight on the edge of the overlook. I'm worried about her and what is in that head of hers. I pull her into me and lie back against the couch; if she won't talk, I will hold her until she does. After a few minutes, her body starts to vibrate, and I can feel her wet tears on my chest through my shirt.

"You want to talk?"

She curls into me more and starts to sob. I don't know what to do or what is wrong, so I just brush her hair out of her face and behind her ear. I really like this shorter haircut. With my index finger, I lift her chin, so she is looking at me, and I kiss her on either side of her eyes while wiping the tears from beneath. I want her to know that I am here, and I want her here, since she doesn't seem to feel wanted. She lifts her hand and touches the side of my face with her palm.

"Why are you so nice to me? I haven't ever done anything to deserve your kindness."

"Kat, you don't have to do anything to deserve it. You don't even know what you do to me. That first day I saw you at the park, you had me with your innocent eyes. I knew I shouldn't want you—you were wearing that school uniform, for God's sake—but you have me crazy, always on my mind, in my head. You would drive me insane every time you came into The Java. I've been waiting for this day, when I could tell you how I feel."

With a shocked look on her face, she pulls away from me, and I all of a sudden feel cold without her heat next to me.

"What are you talking about? We're friends. You can't care for me like that. I have nothing to offer you. I am nothing but a screw-up. I have no friends now, no home to live in, and that just scratches the surface of my problems. I am damaged goods."

"Kat, you have everything I want. Your smile makes my heart melt, your voice gives me chills whenever I hear it, and God, every time I hear Jayce flirt with you or had to hear about him putting the moves on you, I wanted to rip his head off. I want to protect you, and I want to love you."

"You don't even *know* me. How can you love me?"

"I know what you do to me, and I want to get to know you. I want to know all about you, but most of all, right now I want to know what is going on with you, because I feel the need to protect you, but I don't know what from."

"You can't protect me. It's too late, and I have to live with it. There is no saving me from myself."

She gets up suddenly and grabs her duffel and purse and heads for the door. She turns around really fast and says, "Thanks for everything, but I have to go," and then she is gone, running down the stairs and out the door to the alley. By the time I snap out of it and follow, she is gone, nowhere to be seen. *What the hell just happened?*

Chapter Fifteen

Katarina

I run down the alley and around the corner as fast as I can. I'm not sure where I am going, but I have the money from my dad in my account, so I know I can find a cheap place to stay. His words were so sweet and so kind, but he doesn't know what he is getting when it comes to me, and I can't tell him—not now, and maybe not ever. He wants to love me, but I'm not loveable. No one wants me in their life, no one needs me. I'm walking up the street, stuck in my own head, when I feel a hand on my arm. For a second, I hope it's James, but then reality hits me again. This isn't James, it's Trent—again. This can't be happening to me. Before I can turn and go in the opposite direction, I am in a narrow alley between two buildings, pinned to the brick wall, with his hand over my mouth.

"You made me look like a fool tonight and ruined my chance to go after Bren."

I bite his hand and drag in a breath of air. "You made yourself the fool, you bastard. You *raped* me that night. I was a virgin. Stay the fuck away from me and Bren. You are a worthless asshole who needs to be locked away."

His hand slams into my face with such force that I hit the ground with a thud. He is right in my face now, full of rage.

"You bitch! How dare you accuse me of rape? You wanted it just as bad as I did. Keep your mouth shut about this and that night, if you know what is good for you."

He stands and sends his booted foot right into my stomach before turning and walking away. My first thought is my baby, then the pain of the impact. *What is happening to me? How did my life get so fucked up?*

This is not what I thought my eighteenth birthday would be like. It was supposed to be fun, with friends, and fireworks, cake, and music. *What the hell happened to my life?*

I try to get up slowly, gripping the wall for support, but I fall back down to the ground. I start to try and get up again when James runs up to me. His face is tight and angry. I'm too tired to deal with any more anger. He takes one look at my face and brushes his thumb over my cheek where Trent smacked me.

"Kat, what happened to you? Are you all right?" James says.

"I'm fine; it was nothing. I just ran into an old friend who had a grudge."

"At one in the morning? Kat, please come back to my place, at least for tonight."

I hurt, both my mind and my body, and I give in. I let him lead me back to his place. I struggle up the stairs but make it without him realizing how much pain I'm really in. When he opens the door, he leads me to his bed, drops my bag by the foot of it, and walks away. My heart sinks. I was right. No one wants to be around me. Before I can have a complete thought or lie down, he is back with ice wrapped in a towel, and he lays it gently on my face.

"Here, this should make that feel better. Let me go grab some Tylenol for your head, and then I will leave you to sleep."

"Where are you sleeping?" I ask.

"I'll be on the couch, sweetness. As much as it will kill me to be that far from you, that's where I'll be."

As disappointed as I am that he won't be by my side, his words are warm and inviting, and I realize his anger isn't toward me but to the one who harmed me. I take the Tylenol with a glass of water, settle in, and fall asleep fast.

Alone.

James

I get to the main street and have no idea where she disappeared to. Then I hear her raised voice in the distance, and fear rips through me. I run in the direction I thought I heard her and come to an alley where I see her trying to get up off the ground. Rage flies through me the second I see her. I kneel down to her and put my hand to her face, where I notice a bruise starting to form. I know she didn't want to stay with me tonight, but I make her come back to my place; it's too late in the night for her to go anywhere else.

After settling her in with the Tylenol and the makeshift ice pack, I lie on the couch, tossing and turning with my thoughts. *What is going on with her?* I am determined to figure it out in the morning. I need to make her talk to me.

Just as I am actually about to drift off, I hear her moaning. I get up and run into my bedroom and see her curled up in the fetal position. When I look closer, I see tears in her eyes.

"Kat? Are you okay, what's going on?"

"I don't know...my stomach...so much pain."

"What can I do? Do you need to go to the hospital? Never mind, I'm taking you to the hospital. Let's go."

I help her out of my bed and pick her up in my arms. I carry her to my car, set her in the passenger seat, and drive her to the hospital. As I am driving, I notice she is still curled up into herself and crying. I lay my hand on her leg to reaffirm I am there for her, afraid to touch her anywhere else. When we get to the entrance of the ER, I slam the car in park, run around to the passenger side and scoop her into my arms, running through the double doors.

"She needs a doctor; I don't know what's wrong with her. She's in a lot of pain."

A nurse comes over to us, notices the color of her skin and the pain in her eyes, and ushers us to the triage room. I lay her on the bed as the nurse takes her vitals and starts asking questions.

"Sir, can you go to the check-in counter and fill out her paperwork?"

"I don't know how much help I will be, but I can try. Can I bring it back here for Kat to help me fill it out?" I ask.

"Sure. Can you just go get it so that we can move forward and figure out what is wrong with her?"

Chapter Sixteen

Katarina

So much pain.

I am grateful that James had to leave the room so that I could tell the nurse that I am pregnant without him in here.

"Okay, sweetie, what happened to you tonight? I see the bruise on your face, is there anything else you want to tell me?"

"I'm eleven weeks pregnant and was assaulted in an alley tonight around one; my attacker kicked me in the stomach." I nod in the direction James left. "He doesn't know I'm pregnant."

"He is going to know before too long. We are going to have to check that baby out, so unless we don't let him back in here, and I don't think that will make him happy, you may want to talk to him."

James comes into the room with a clipboard in hand and a weird look on his face. The nurse excuses herself, and behind James's back, gives me a pointed look. "I'll be back in a few minutes."

"So, I just realized I don't know anything about you besides your first name and age. We need to change this; I need to know you.

Everything about you. I wish you would talk to me—let me into that pretty little head of yours."

"Funny you should say that, I do have something I need to tell you, and it's better you hear from me than the doctors or nurses here."

He grabs my hand and looks right into my eyes. "Tell me, anything, *everything*. What is going on?"

"James, I'm pregnant. I am about eleven weeks along—" A sob escapes. "And I am scared out of my mind right now. That jerk who hit me in the face kicked me in the stomach, too."

He wraps his arms around me, puts a kiss on my forehead like he has done before, and then looks into my eyes. "Kat, it's going to be okay," he says, a steely edge to his voice. "I am here for you no matter what, but I want to talk to you more about this later, once we know you're okay."

How did I deserve someone like James in my life? How did I get so lucky? At least for the moment he is sweet and kind, but I see darkness behind the light with my news. I am lucky that he doesn't seem to judge me, but he does seem angry—full of rage. I have a feeling that later I will feel the wrath of his anger and be assaulted by a thousand questions. I am not sure if I am ready to tell him everything, but I want to. He is the only person I truly want to know my truth.

♡

James

Who the hell got her pregnant and when? I would have pegged her for a virgin. Eleven weeks ago, she got pregnant... I will find out more, but right now, I need to be here for her—she's so scared. I wrap my arms around her and kiss her forehead and make it known that *she* is what is important to me at this point. I think she sees what lies behind the kindness and concern. I think she sees the rage and the anger. I just hope she doesn't think it's toward her.

I start asking her the questions on the papers while we wait for the nurse to return, holding her hand the entire time. I am there for her, and I want her to know it.

Chapter Seventeen

Katarina

The nurse comes back into the room with a cart of monitors and straps.

"Are the forms filled out?"

James hands her the clipboard and immediately goes back to holding my hand.

The nurse looks at me with approval and proceeds to tell me we have to hook me up to these monitors on my stomach and starts strapping them to me. I hear this faint thumping sound from the monitor and ask, "Is that the heartbeat?"

"Yes, and it is sounding strong. That is a good sign, Kat. We are going to monitor you for a little bit while we wait for the doctor to arrive. Then we will go get the ultrasound tech and take a look at your baby. How is the pain now?"

With tears in my eyes, I answer, "It isn't as strong like before, but it is still there, more of a dull feeling now."

I look over at James, and he still has that look on his face. I don't know what it is exactly, but I do recognize the look of concern etched into his face. He hasn't let go of my hand the entire time. I wish I understood why he's being so nice. I know he said he wants to love me, but I'm no one to love. I'm not convinced my own mother loves me, and my father definitely doesn't feel anything beyond obligation. Right now, I can't think of anything to do with James, so I concentrate on the feeling I feel the most—hope. The sound of the heartbeat in the room just made it real. I have a baby inside me, and I have to do whatever I can to protect it.

The nurse continues to take my vitals and look at the monitor and has a happy look on her face. I hope that means that everything is okay—that everything is going to be okay.

"I'll go get the doctor and see if the ultrasound machine is free. Have you seen your baby yet?"

"No, I had an appointment set up for next week."

"Well, looks like you are going to get a treat today."

The nurse walks out, and James looks at me, like he is looking through my soul.

"Kat, when we find out everything is okay with you and the baby, you are coming back to my house. You can stay with me for as long as you need to."

"James, I can't stay with you. You hardly know me. I hardly know you! And I'm pregnant with some other guy's baby. No, just no. I can't."

"Yes, you can, and you will." He gets a look on his face, and this time I recognize it for what it is: stubbornness.

The doctor knocks on the door and comes into my room. *Saved by the doc!*

"Katarina, hi, I am Dr. Knox." He shakes my hand as he introduces himself to me. "So, from what I understand, you were assaulted tonight and kicked in the stomach. Is this correct?"

I take a glance over at James. The stubborn look is gone, replaced with pure rage.

"Yes, that is correct. I started having severe pain a few hours later and came straight here."

"Well, it looks like the baby has a strong heartbeat," he says as he looks at the long paper coming from the monitor machine. "Do you still have severe pain, or has it subsided?"

"The pain comes and goes, but it's not nearly as bad as it was before."

"Well, I like the looks of your vitals and your baby's heartrate, so let's move on to the ultrasound. Let me just go get the tech with the machine."

He walks out the door, and the second the door shuts, I feel the anger coming off of James. His hand tightens around mine, and he looks right into my eyes.

"You never said he kicked you. Who was it?"

"No one you need to worry about. No one that needs to know I am pregnant. No one that I ever want to see again."

"We will talk more about this later once we are home."

Home. I like the way that sounds, but I can't play house with this man. I can't let myself believe that it's possible. I can't tell him my secrets. He will never look at me the same again.

The doctor knocks on the door again, and a technician walks in behind him with the machine. I am excited and terrified at the same time. *What if something is wrong with the baby? I can't wait to see the little one growing in my tummy.*

"Okay, Katarina, let's take a look at your baby. The technician will be doing the ultrasound, but I want to be in here to see what is going on. Now, you said there was no bleeding, just the severe cramping, correct?"

"Yes, just the cramping," I reply.

The tech introduces herself as Amy and then asks me to lift my shirt so she can remove the monitors and put some cold goo on my abdomen. I also have to lower my yoga pants to a point that I'm a little embarrassed about in front of James, but he seem unfazed.

"This may be a little cold," she says as she squirts the goo on my belly.

I cringe. "Just a little."

She starts rubbing her wand across my stomach and turns the monitor so we can see a little better. I hear the heartbeat almost immediately and crank my head to see the screen. This little shape that looks almost like a little human appears, but the torso is so small, almost equal to the size of the little one's head. It's so small and innocent. I start to tear up at the sight. I take the hand that isn't in James's and cover my mouth. "Oh, my God."

I feel James tighten his grip on my hand for a second, as if this moment is meaningful for him, too. The tech continues to move her wand around my stomach pressing down to the point it's almost painful to be able to see everything around the baby and the baby itself. She seems to be snapping some pictures and has a slight smile on her face as she looks toward the doctor.

"Well, is everything okay?" I ask.

The doctor writes something down on his form and looks up to me. "Everything seems to look okay. The baby is healthy and doing just fine. I would recommend that you go home, drink some water, and stay off your feet for a few days. If you have any bleeding, call your doctor immediately or come back here, if it's really bad. I'll have the nurse come back in with your discharge paperwork and let you finish up with Amy. You both have a good morning, and I am glad everything is okay."

The doctor leaves, and Amy turns to me with a handful of pictures in one hand and a towel in the other.

"First off, let's get you all cleaned up, and then you can have these to take with you."

She wipes my stomach with the towel and pulls my shirt down before handing me the pictures in her hand. My first photos of my baby. If I thought the heartbeat made it real, seeing my baby makes it even more real. For the first time since I found out I was pregnant,

I have something besides fear and dread in my heart. I'm truly excited for this little one, in spite of everything else. I have no home anymore, and no job. Thankfully, I have some money in my account, but it won't last long.

My nurse comes back in with my discharge paperwork, and she and Amy send me on my way. Everything just got real for me.

James

We leave the hospital, and I lead her to my car. I am so full of different emotions, but besides the concern I feel, I have rage building every step I take. I don't know how it happened, but I fell for this girl sitting next to me. The worse thing with that is that I don't think she feels the same way about me, or if she does, she is hiding it well.

I want to know who attacked her in that alley, and I want to know why. She said that he couldn't find out that she was pregnant. *Who did get her pregnant?* So many questions and very few answers, but I hate to get her riled up when she's obviously hurt. Once I pull out of the parking lot, I grab her hand again and hold it. I have hardly let go of it all night. The sun is starting to rise, and I need to get to the coffee shop soon to open it up. The first thing I need to do is get Kat to my apartment and settled in—once I convince her to stay with me.

"Once we get home, I have to go to the coffee shop to open, but I'll be back as soon as I can. I want you to settle in and rest, like the doctor said. No argument, okay?"

She frowns. "I'll stay for today, but I have to find somewhere else to go tomorrow."

"You really don't, you can stay with me for as long as you need.

It really isn't a problem." I try to keep my tone reasonable, but I'm struggling.

"I really can't stay with you. I just can't."

Reminding myself again that she's been through a lot in the last twenty-four hours, I decide to take what I can get. For now. "Fine, but we will talk about it later, after you have gotten some rest."

I park the car behind my building and run around to get the door for Kat and help her out. We walk slowly up to my apartment, and I get her settled on the couch with a bottle of water, a blanket, and the TV remote.

"I have to go downstairs and get the cafe opened. As soon as Kelly shows up, I will come back up here to check on you." I put a kiss to her forehead and walk toward the door.

I look back at her, and she has a look on her face like she's afraid, or maybe confused. Right now, though, I'm relieved to have her safe at home. My home.

Chapter Eighteen

Katarina

I am in his house; it feels right, but then, on the other hand, it feels so wrong. He doesn't know the real me. He doesn't know what happened. I have so many things wrong with me, and I don't deserve this kindness. I don't deserve his love in any form. I need to get out of here before he gets back. So, I decide I need to call Bren. I know she is pissed at me, but I also think it's time I fill her in on my secrets, make her understand that it isn't my fault I got pregnant with Trent's baby, that I didn't even want to have sex with him. I need to tell her what he did to me, so she stays away from him. I pick up my phone, knowing that it is early, but hoping that she will understand. I'm not even sure she'll answer my call.

I dial her number and listen to it ring and ring, and right when I think that she won't answer, I get a very groggy, "Hello?"

"Hey, I know you're pissed at me, but I need you. Can you come get me?"

"Kat, it is too damn early. I just went to bed a couple hours ago, what do you want? I'm pretty tired of coming to your rescue."

"I'm at James' apartment above the coffee shop. I need to talk to you. Bren, please. I can't be here."

"Why not? What trouble have you gotten yourself into now?"

"I was at the hospital last night. Please, can you come get me?"

"Are you okay? What happened?"

"I am okay, but I need to make you understand what is going on with me. I am ready to talk to only you."

"So, talk."

"Bren, I would really rather have this conversation in person. Park in the alley behind The Java, and I will meet you. I don't care what you're wearing—I just need you. I need to get out of here. You were right, he's interested in me, and I can't do this with him. Please just come and get me," I beg.

"I'll be there as soon as I can. I will text you when I am near."

"Thank you, I love you."

"I'll be there soon," she answers back without much feeling in her voice.

As I hang up with her, I can hear her clattering around in the bathroom. I'm sure some people would take what James is offering and never think twice. He wants to love me, but I can't have him do that. I can't have him love me the way I am. I have nothing to offer; I would just drag him down.

Twenty minutes later, I get a text just as James comes in the door. *Shit*, I think to myself, *he wasn't supposed to come back up here.* I was supposed to just slink away without a trace.

"Kat, how ya doing?" he calls from the door.

"Good, much better. There is almost no pain at all anymore." I get up and go to the bathroom to text Bren back.

K: Change of plans. Come in the second door in the alley, upstairs top floor.

Bren: Okay be right there

I walk back out to the living room right as she knocks on the door. I grab my bag and walk right by him, ignoring the confused look on his face as I go straight to the door. I don't say a word to him as I walk out and down the stairs with Bren following me.

"What was that about, K? He looked like you just kicked his puppy."

"He didn't know I was leaving. I'm no good for him. You will understand soon enough why that is."

"Okay, if you say so."

We get into Bren's car, and she drives away. I look behind me to see him standing at the door, looking sad and angry and something else I can't quite place. I turn back around with a tear in my eye and force him from my head.

"Where to, K?" Bren asks.

"Anywhere we can talk in private will work. It's a nice day. Why don't we go to the park by your house? The one by the water." *The one he saved me from last night.*

We get to the park and I decide I need to walk around in the open space for this, so I walk toward the water where James found me the night before. I stand there in silence as Bren comes up to me and stands next to me, not speaking. A few minutes go by, and I take a huge breath, preparing myself to tell all.

"Bren? I don't know where to start."

"How about at the beginning?"

"Okay, well, you know that first party you brought me to? That is where it all changed."

"Go on."

"Well, that night I did too much of everything. Everything was new. I was drinking anything they handed me, smoking weed, and I snorted coke for the first time. I felt pretty, and different. I had never held the attention of a boy before—I was a virgin, actually. That night, Trent started talking to me, and after a few minutes, he started kissing me. It was nice at first. He started to touch me, and even that was okay. But then everything changed. He changed. He got rough and pushed me down on the couch. I was so messed up I barely knew where I was. Hell, until last night, I wasn't even sure of his name. I tried to push him off of me, but I failed. Bren, Trent raped me, and he's been following me the past couple weeks, too. This is why I reacted the way I did last night." I have tears streaming down my face at this point, and I take a chance and look at Bren's face to see her reaction. She has tears forming in her eyes. "I didn't want this. I didn't want my first time to be like this, and I sure as hell didn't want to end up pregnant. I remember it was him, though; I can't get his face out of my nightmares."

Bren has a look of shock and sadness on her face. Maybe it's pity, I don't know.

"This is what has been going on with you for so long? Why didn't you ever say anything to me? I love you like a sister. I am always on your side—well, except for last night. I was being selfish last night." She wraps her arms around me, and we sink to the ground together. Then, while wiping the tears from her eyes, she asks, "What happened to your face, anyway? And why did you go to the hospital?"

"James found me, here, actually, sitting on the edge of the cliff. He saved me from I don't know what—jumping, falling accidently on purpose, I don't know, but he did. I wasn't right in my head last night. He took me back to his place and told me exactly what you thought he would tell me. He believes he is falling in love with me. I freaked out and took off, and Trent found me and dragged me into an alley. Then he got in my face and told me not to tell anyone about that night. He smacked me in the face so hard I fell, and then when I was down on the ground, he kicked me in the stomach. James found me again and took me back to his place and put me in his bed. I fell asleep soon after that but woke up with sharp pains in my stomach. James brought me to the ER."

Bren pulls back and looks me right in the eyes. "Trent did this to you. Oh, my God, I never would have suspected he would be like that, do something like that. I can't believe I wanted to hook up with him, and I got pissed at you about him last night. I wish you would've told me about all of this sooner. Last night never would have happened, and you would have been safe in my house, I'm so sorry Kat."

She wraps her arms around me again, and we sit there crying together for a while.

"We have to tell someone about this. You can't live in fear of him because he keeps popping up. What if he does some serious damage the next time he corners you? Or does this to someone else?"

"I'm terrified of what he'll do if he finds out I'm pregnant and it's his. I also don't want anyone to know this happened to me. I don't want James to know. It isn't fair to him. James just needs to walk away from me, as much as I would love to let him love me."

"What did they say at the hospital this morning? Is everything okay?"

"I am supposed to rest and stay off my feet for a few days, and James wanted me to stay with him. James knows I'm pregnant. I feel like a fool. I could have had a nice thing with him, and it's ruined. My life is ruined. *He* ruined my life." I point to my stomach. "But this part I wouldn't change." I remember the ultrasound. "Oh! I have pictures of the baby."

"Let me see them!" she squeals, like an excited schoolgirl who just got her first date.

I pull out the strip of pictures and show her. She gets as emotional about them as I did when I saw my baby on the monitor.

"As much as this is exciting, we need to do something. Your mom left this morning on her honeymoon thinking that you were at my house. She cares, Kat. I just don't think she reacted the best way. For now, you can stay with me at my house, but we will have to tell my parents something. You will start to show soon. Actually, you are already starting to look a little on the fat side," she jokes.

"Gee, thanks! Give me a few more days. We will talk to your parents soon, I promise."

I have my best friend back, and I'm starting to feel wanted again. I felt wanted by James, but that's not for me. Bren has been with me from the beginning, and now she knows the truth. I feel better now that I have talked to her. We go back to her car to go to her house. Once I am in and seated, I look at my phone; I have a ton of text messages from a contact named J<3. A glance at the texts tells me this is James. *When did I get his number?* Then I realize he must have put his number in my phone at some point, because the first message is from me, to him, and I didn't send it.

K: <3
J<3: why did you leave? Are you okay?
J<3: Kat where are you?
J<3: Please come back and talk to me
J<3: Kat I'm worried about you
J<3: Kat please talk to me I'm going crazy here
J<3: Talk to me, I care about you

I cry as I read that last message. I turn my phone off as Bren looks over to me with worry in her eyes.

"You okay?"

"No. How can he care anything about me when he doesn't even know me?"

"You're going to have to talk to him. I don't think there is a way around it at this point, but not now. Right now, we need to get you to my house and get some rest, both of us."

I turn my head to look out the window as she pulls onto the main road toward her house. We are at her house within minutes, and then she is ushering me into her room and onto the bed like I am a fragile vase.

"Go to sleep. I'm going to go get a drink, and I will be back to take a nap with you. "

I lie there with my eyes wide open—I don't know when I will sleep again; I have too many nightmares to contend with. I do eventually fall asleep, and when I wake up, I realize it is after lunchtime, and Bren is sitting on the edge of the bed with some water and Tylenol for the headache she assumes I have. I take the Tylenol and drink the water then I decide I should turn my phone back on. I have one more message then I did before.

J<3: Please talk to me

I reply back to him this time with a simple sentence.

K<3: I'm fine with Bren

I hit send and turn my phone off again. He isn't something I feel like dealing with today. I'm not sure when I *will* be ready to deal with him, in fact. I may not know him well, but the parts I do know, I *do* kinda love. I just can't deal with that right now.

♡♡

James

After a stunned realization that she's leaving without a single word, I go running out the door, but I'm too late—the car door shuts and they are off. I don't even have time to yell after her. She said she would give me today. She said she would stay. *What changed?*

I try texting her over and over with no answer. While she was sleeping the night before, I put my number into her phone and sent myself a text, so I had hers. This girl is driving me crazy. I finally text her once last time, telling her that I care about her, and a few hours later I get a response back.

K<3: I'm fine with Bren

Well, at least I know she's safe, but I still want to know why she left. I leave it alone for now and decide to go back to work and try to get my head together. This girl has me so wound up that if I don't love her, I might hate her for it.

I walk into the cafe and head over to the counter to make myself a coffee. I feel my employees looking at me, but they don't say a word. I must be emitting a pretty ominous vibe. I go into the office and try to work. Instead, I sit there and start thinking about the past twenty-four hours and how horribly wrong they went.

I woke up excited yesterday, thinking that I was going to be able to finally act on my feelings for Kat and give her the present I had for her: a beautiful, small, emerald pendant on a delicate chain. I never got the chance to give it to her because of everything that happened at the party, and then when I was talking to her last night she spooked and ran. Add in her getting hurt and then going to the ER, and finding out she's pregnant, and I was a little distracted. I don't know how I feel about that. I don't like it, but I want to be there for her. I want to find the guy that hurt her and smash his face in and bring him to his knees. I want to find the guy that got her pregnant and ask why he isn't helping her. I want to hold her in my arms and never let her go.

I want, I want, I want.

I wish I understood why I feel so connected to her—why I can't get her out of my head. She is beautiful and sweet, and now her eyes have gone dark, when before they were bright and full of life. I want to be the one to put the life back into her eyes.

I'm probably not what she needs, though. I have my own demons. My parents are dead, and my life before this one wasn't pretty. I was able to snap out of the cycle of drugs and partying as soon as I heard they died, but I still have bad people in my life. I try to stay away from them the best I can, but my parents brought me into that world the second they left it.

My parents lived in Boston; they were connected to a mob family in Eastie —and not connected in a good way. Both of my parents were known by the "Family"—my mom was a waitress, and my dad did the books for this club. The problem was, my mom caught the eye of one of the family members, and there was no saying no to him. He wanted her, married or not. This was before I was born—about nine months, as a matter of fact. So, I later found out my dad wasn't my dad, and my mom fell in love with this mobster. My dad was left to fend for himself, never gaining any rank. My home life was a lie, and their death didn't make things any easier. My biological father wants me to move to Boston and be a part of that life. I have refused him many times. After my parents died, I took the money my mother had stashed away, got myself cleaned up, and bought this building. I started a fresh life. Still, to this day, I regularly have Family members stop in and check on me, asking the never-ending question of when I will join the Family and the never-ending answer of, *I won't be.* I don't want to be connected to them in this way and have taken great pains to minimize how many people in my life know about them. I can't let them know about Kat. I can't let them into her world, and if I want her in my world, then they will be in hers.

I sit there, mind whirling, and realize I won't be getting any work done, so I finish my coffee and walk back out to the café, where I see Jayce walking in the door.

"Hey, boss, awesome party last night at Bren's house, wasn't it?"

"I didn't stay long, but it looked like a lot of fun."

"I noticed. What happened? Both you and Kat disappeared last night."

"Kat wasn't feeling good, so I took her down to the park."

He had a look like he wanted to punch me in the face, then it disappeared.

I knew he wanted to get together with her, but I also knew it wasn't going to happen.

"How did you end up taking her?" he questions.

"I ran into her after the squabble with her mom, and she wanted to get away and asked me to get her out of there," I lie. "So, I took her to the park, and we talked for a little while. I brought her back to Bren's house."

I sure as hell can't tell this guy what all happened last night. I can't tell him that I think I'm in love with her, and I sure as hell can't declare her mine. Not yet. Maybe not ever.

"I'm heading out for the rest of the day. Call if you need anything, Jayce. I'll be back later to close up." I always do the books, and I always do the deposit. That is something the Family taught me: don't trust anyone with your money. I head out the door and start walking. I need to get my head on straight, and sometimes physical activity really helps me work things out mentally.

Chapter Nineteen

Katarina

Bren pushes me into her bathroom to take a shower, turns the water on for me and grabs a towel.

"Take a shower, K. You'll feel better." And then she leaves me alone.

I take my clothes off and step into the shower, letting the water flow over me. As the water cascades down my body, the tears start to flow, too. I can't stop them; they just keep coming. I look down at my stomach and notice I have some bruising. I don't even want to look at my face. With everything going on, I am just spent. I sit in the shower and sob for I don't know how long. I feel the water start to cool and quickly run some conditioner through my hair and wash my body then rinse everything. Stepping out of the shower, I wrap the towel around me and avoid the mirror. In the bedroom, I notice Bren has laid out some clothes for me—a pair of yoga pants and a T-shirt I didn't realize I had. It belongs to James, I must have shoved it in my bag when I was at his place last night. I get dressed and head out to the kitchen, where I hear Bren talking with her mom. They both turn and look at me, but Tina gasps. Then it hits me: my face. *Shit.*

"Hi, is it really that bad?"

"Oh, sweetheart, what happened to your face?" Tina asks.

"She had a run-in last night, Mom, after she left here with James."

There is steel in Tina's voice when she asks, "Did he do this to you?"

"No, it most definitely wasn't James," Bren assures her.

Bren takes a look at me, and at this point I know we have to tell her mom. I don't want to, but I don't have a choice. I look at Bren and nod my head; she knows that it is okay to speak.

"Mom, we have a lot to tell you, but please listen to everything."

"Okay, I will listen. Start talking. I am responsible for Kat while her mom is out of town. Do I need to call her?"

"My mom knows part of what is going on, and really, that was what our fight was about last night. She kicked me out of the house Friday when she found out. So, I guess I am responsible for myself now."

With a look of shock on her face, her eyes pop open wide. "She did *what?* Why would she do that?"

"She doesn't know the entire story. I wasn't ready to tell it. Heck, I almost lost Bren over not telling her the truth. That is why I left last night, and James found me at the park down the street. I was with James last night at his apartment. You both were right. He said he wants to love me. I got spooked and took off from his building, and I was attacked. The guy hit me in the face, and kicked me in the stomach. He left me on the ground. James found me again as I was trying to get up off the ground. He brought me back to his place and put me to bed. I wouldn't tell him anything, especially with the rage I saw in his eyes."

Bren urges me to keep going. "K, you need to start at the beginning. You need to tell my mom what happened, even if I get into deep shit with it, too."

I take a deep breath and continued.

"Bren took me to a party about eleven weeks ago at an apartment downtown. There were tons of people there, and a lot of drugs. We were drinking, and smoking some pot, and then when someone offered us a line of coke, we decided to do it."

With a very audible gasp, she asks, *"You did what?"*

"Mom, yell at me later. K is what is important here. I haven't done it again, and that was my first time too. This is my fault; I left her alone." I see the regret in her eyes and shake my head at her to communicate that it isn't her fault, but I can tell she doesn't believe me.

"Go on, Kat."

"Okay, so I was really messed up. I could barely navigate at all, so I took a seat on one of the couches in the corner, away from everyone. This guy sat down next to me and started flirting. Bren knows him a little—his name is Trent. I never get attention from boys, and I liked it, at first. He started kissing me, making me feel wanted. Then before I knew what was going on, he was on top of me. I wasn't strong enough to push him off, and no one could hear me yelling over the music. He raped me."

And that makes two people that know what had happened to me. I sit there, tears streaming down my face, and Tina comes over and wraps her arms around me. I bury my face into her and sob harder. Bren is next to come over and wrap her arms around us. We stay like that for a few minutes. Tina backs away slowly and looks me in the eyes.

"Kat, we have to go to the police. We have to report both incidents. We have to do it today."

I yell, *"No!* We can't. I can't do that. He can't know. *Bren, he can't know."*

Tina looks at us, startled and confused. "What aren't you telling me?"

Bren takes this one for me. "Kat's pregnant, Mom. She doesn't want him to know. I actually suspect he has an idea that she is pregnant, since he kicked her in the stomach last night. He has been stalking her, and I doubt he found her by accident after she left James's apartment. He threatened her, and Kat is very scared, Mom. I'm scared for her."

Bren comes back to me and wraps her arms around me, once again giving me comfort. I look over to her mom, who is now shedding tears.

"Mom, can Kat just stay here for this week? Let her figure things out? We can keep her safe here, and the ER doctor said she needs to stay off her feet for a few days anyway after she was there last night for severe cramping. She and the baby are fine, but he wants her to rest."

"I will leave this alone for the time being. Yes, you can stay here, but you can't live in fear of this guy forever. He will figure out you have his baby. He will make your life a living hell, but with all that said, I will be here for you. I don't understand why your mom would kick you out over being raped and getting pregnant." Tina pauses and then speaks slowly. "Unless…she doesn't know the part about you being raped, does she?"

I hang my head in shame. "No, she doesn't. You and Bren are the only ones that I have told. Mom and James know I am pregnant, but they don't know that part. I can't tell James. I just can't. My mom wasn't ready to hear me out, and after her response, I didn't want to tell her. Heck, until this morning, I didn't want to tell anyone what had happened. I guess I will have to tell my mom now, but no way will I be living with her and her new husband. I would rather live in a sketchy room in the Old Port and work my ass off then live with them."

With a smirk on her face, Bren replies to my outburst. "There is always James. He offered you a place to live."

"No, *just no*. I can't do that to him. I can't tell him this; I'd rather he thinks I was a slut than tell him I was raped."

"Well, isn't that mature of you." Bren looks at me pointedly.

At this point, I am drained, so I ignore her comment and tell them I need to go rest. Bren comes with me, and we get comfy on her couch in front of the TV.

"You both need to eat something. We have plenty of leftovers; I'll make you a plate." Tina yells in from the kitchen.

We turn on Netflix and find a new rom-com to take our minds off reality. A few minutes later, Tina brings in some plates of food. "Kat, have you thought about talking to someone about what happened to you? Maybe a counselor that specialized in rape trauma? Even if you don't want to go to the police, to avoid attention from Trent, I think you should talk to someone."

"I haven't even thought about it. I've been trying to move on, keep it all to myself, but the nightmares won't go away. Maybe I should talk to someone."

"I can look into some resources for you today and see what I can find. Right now, just eat something and relax."

"Thanks, Tina."

Bren and I relax the rest of the day, watching movies. I still have the look James gave me as we drove off stuck my head, and I feel bad about leaving like that. Tomorrow, I will talk to him. Tomorrow is a new day, and tomorrow I will conquer my life. Well, one step at a time, but tomorrow is still a new day. I block out James from my head and eat some food and watch movies with my best friend.

James

It has now been three days since I have heard from her, and I'm losing my mind. I wish I had Bren's number so that I could check on Kat. I broke down today and drove past Bren's house, but I didn't stop. Bren's car is parked in the driveway, and I just hope that Kat is with her. I go back to my apartment and park in the back alley, where I see two guys in suits leaned against my building.

"You need to come with us; your father wants to see you," the guy on the right says.

I sigh and nod. It's pointless to try to evade them. *Why does he want to see me now?* Nothing has changed: I want to continue to live this life I have made for myself.

They usher me to the back of a black sedan and drive away. I have no idea where we are going, but he must be close, because we aren't heading to the highway toward Boston. They park in front of the Majesty Hotel and one guy gets out, comes to my door, and pulls me out of the car. He leads me into the hotel—I don't even have a chance to look around the lobby; we go straight to the elevators. He swipes a card over the panel that allows us to go to the penthouse. Neither of us speak on the ride up. When the door opens, we are greeted by two more guys in black suits at the entrance of the penthouse. Inside I am directed to a chair and told to sit. He goes to another room, and, a few minutes later, comes back out with the man that calls himself my dad. He is no father to me; he is just the guy that manipulated my mother and got her pregnant.

He gets straight to the point. "So, I hear you have a girl in your life. Katarina, is it?"

How does he know anything about her, and what does he want with her?

"I'm sorry, I don't know what you are talking about."

"Don't you lie to me," he booms. "I have eyes and ears on you at all times."

I sigh. "What do you want?"

"I want you in Boston with me, and if I have to use her to get it, I will. In fact, I already have."

"What are you talking about? Why is it so important that I be by your side? I have nothing to offer you besides the blood I share with you."

"You have plenty to offer me. I need you to take over the business. You are next in line, *my son*," he grinds out.

"You don't sound so happy about that," I comment. "I'm sure you can find someone else to take over. Another hidden child, maybe?"

He hesitates a second, almost unrecognizable to anyone else, but I catch it. I am almost certain there *is* someone else. Interesting.

"You are it. You would be set for life: money, girls, luxury. Anything you want it can be yours if you just join me in Boston."

"I don't need any of that. Why are you stepping down? You must be dying," I say with laugh.

"Actually, I am. I found out about three months ago that I was going to die. I have cancer. You are all that I have left, and I need you to take over."

I'm stunned at his admission, but it doesn't change much for me.

"Yeah, I'm sorry you're sick and all, but I am not your replacement. I am nothing like you. I don't want to be like you. I like my life the way it is. Find someone else. "

"You don't understand. There can be no one else. I can't just hand this over to anyone. It has to be you. This is a family business, and I can't have anyone else looking after it. Like I said, I'll use the girl if I need to. I've already set the plan in motion."

I grind out, "What have you done to her?"

"Does Trent ring a bell?"

"You sent him after her? How do you know Trent?"

"He works for me. Well, his father works for me, and now he does too, because I needed him."

"I will not work for you; I will not become you. Find someone else and stay away from Kat."

"Sorry, son, that isn't going to happen. I need you. If you want your girl to stay in one piece, you better think twice about saying no to me. I will be back in two weeks to get you and bring you to Boston. Find someone to manage your business and get your shit packed. Two weeks, son."

Now would be the perfect time to find out I have a brother somewhere in the world, someone who is just like him. I leave the penthouse on my own. It isn't too far from my café, and I walk straight into the office. I need to find this person he is hiding. I will not leave here and go to Boston to become the head of a mob family. It isn't who I am, and I won't let it happen.

I get on the computer and look for a private investigator. I need to find who he is hiding, like yesterday. After making a few calls, I have a meeting set up for tonight at six. This has to end now. This has to end before Kat is hurt even more by the man who calls himself my father.

At 5:30, I grab my things and walk out the door of my cafe to go meet with the investigator. I knock on his door when I arrive and am greeted immediately.

"Hey, you must be James. I'm Grant, nice to meet you."

I shake his hand and he motions for me to sit. I notice he's about my age and height with dark hair, he seems nice enough but has an edge to his voice like he loves a challenge. I get the feeling right off the bat that he'll be a good fit for the job.

"What can I do for you?"

"Well, I was visited this afternoon by my biological father. He has been threatening the ones close to me, and I need it to stop. I need to find out if I have any other living blood relatives."

"Why is that?"

"My biological father is the head of the Milano family in Boston. We don't have a cordial relationship. He is apparently dying, and he wants me to take over, and I don't want that title. I have made a good life for myself away from them. I need to find out if I have a biological brother who can take the head, so I don't have to."

"What information can you give me?"

"My mother was a waitress at a strip club, The Lucky Lady, in Boston. She had an affair with Al Milano. My mother and father moved here to Maine. When they died, I got my life together, and that's when Al started to invade mine, trying to bring me in. He lives in a brownstone on Beacon Hill and has always been in the Boston area. I have mostly avoided him up until now. He is causing some major trouble for me and wants me to be in Boston in two weeks to take over."

"So, we have to work fast. I know a little bit about the Milano Family. I can probably find what you are looking for. I assume you want a rush on this with the time restriction?"

"Yes, I will do whatever I have to, whatever it takes to get me out of this mess. Can you help me?"

"I believe I can. I will start immediately. If I remember correctly, the Milano family owns The Lucky Lady, so it shouldn't be too hard to find something out soon."

"Thank you, I will wait to hear from you."

I leave the meeting as he starts working on finding out if I have a sibling. I have so much going on in my head right now that I decide to take a walk instead of going back to work. Before I know it, I find myself on the opposite side of the city. I don't live in a huge city, but the fact that I am so distracted I walked from one end to the other says a lot.

I make my way back to the cafe to close up for the night, and Jayce is there starting to wipe down the counters and clean the machines, since we close in forty-five minutes.

"Hey, how was the night?"

"It was actually pretty slow. I already have this machine cleaned for the night," he says as he makes one last wipe with his rag.

"It will probably pick up tomorrow with the weekend coming.

I'm going to go start in on the paperwork. Just come get me when the door is locked."

"You got it."

I leave Jayce to his closing duties and walk back to the office to start in on my paperwork for the day. At closing time, Jayce comes back to the office to let me know that the door is locked, and I walk out front for the cash drawer.

We blast some music as we both finish up what we need to do, and I lose myself in the music. I need to figure out how to get myself out of this position with the man who calls me son, and I need to get my girl back and keep her safe. Jayce pokes his head in the office door as I'm finishing up balancing the cash drawer with the register totals. "I got everything done and shiny for you. I am going to head out now."

I get up and lock the door behind him, and then go and finish the work I need to get done. I close up shop and head to my apartment. I'm exhausted and quickly fall asleep, in spite of thoughts of Kat and my father swirling in my head.

I wake up to the sound of my phone ringing the next morning.

"Hello?"

"James, I think I found something." It's the investigator.

"Looks like you may have a brother three years older than you in New York. From what I found, he doesn't seem to be a nice guy. It looks like he may be affiliated with a family there, the Castillos. His mom was also a waitress at The Lucky Lady. It looks like your dad has a habit with the ladies there."

"What do you mean 'he is affiliated with the Castillo family?'"

"His uncle is in the ranks with them. Low on the totem pole, but still a part of them. Do you know anything about this family? Where do they sit with the Milano family?"

"Honestly, I haven't paid any attention. I want nothing to do with either family. How do I find him?"

"You go to New York. I haven't pinpointed a location. His name is Jackson Dewitt, and his mother is Jamie Dewitt. The uncle is Jacob Cantinilo. That is all I have found out for you"

"Thanks, man. Call if you find out anything else. I will be heading to New York tomorrow."

I hang up with the investigator and go to my computer to book a one-way ticket to New York. Once I get a bag packed, I open my laptop and search the Castillo family to find out more about them. I need to refine my area to look in New York—it's a big city, after all.

I don't find much on the family, so I search the Castillo family and Milano family to see if there is any connection. I get a hit; they apparently are connected way down the ranks. Jacob Cantinilo is married to my aunt—my dad's sister. This is exactly what I need to know, and I hope to work it in my favor.

After a restless night's sleep, I get up and open the café. Once things get going for the day and I have my morning workers in, I head to my office and call Jayce. He is my second-in-command, and as much as I hate it, and I need him.

"Jayce. Sorry to wake you, but I need you to do me a favor this next week."

"What is it, boss?"

"I have to go out of town, so I need you to step up and manage the shop while I am gone. I need you to open and close. We need to work the schedule so you can do that. Can you come in in like an hour?"

"Yeah. Let me get showered and dressed, and I will be there."

"See you then."

An hour later, Jayce shows up and heads straight for the espresso machine. I probably would do the same thing if I was rudely woken up. Once he has his coffee, he comes back to the office, where I am already working on the schedule.

"Hey, boss."

"Hey, Jayce. Thanks for coming in. I appreciate you helping me out this next week. I think I have the schedule worked out for you, although it looks like there may be a couple times for closing you may be alone. I think you can handle it, though."

"I got it, boss. What is so important that you are rushing out of here so fast?"

"I just have some things I need to take care of. I should be back in a week. I'll call you and check in every day. Oh, and here is where I am weird about this: I don't allow anyone to do the books or handle the deposit. If you can just take all the paperwork from the register and the money, and put it into the safe, that would be great. I just need you to leave two hundred in the register each night and the rest in the safe. You can make change if you need to, but I will work the books for the week when I get back."

"Got it, boss. Don't worry about a thing; I got you covered."

"Thanks, Jayce. Now, I have got to go make the deposit and head to the airport. Call me if you need anything. I will see you in about a week."

Chapter Twenty

Katarina

I haven't left the house in three days. I don't want to face the world, but I have to do something. I have to figure out the things that I can control, so I grab my laptop from my bag and start to look for apartments. Nothing big, and nothing too expensive. After an hour of looking, I find a cute little loft apartment, and it is actually in the Old Port district right up the street from James. I get excited and make the call. Six hundred and fifty dollars a month, with no deposit, and all utilities included. *Perfect*. I get the landlord on the line and set up an appointment for the following day to take a look at it. Bren walks in the room and sees the look of excitement on my face.

"Why so excited?"

"I have an appointment in the morning to look at a loft apartment in the Old Port. It's $650 a month, all utilities included, and no deposit."

"Well, that sounds like a good deal. What time are we taking a look?"

"Tomorrow morning at ten."

"That is doable, and we can stop in and get a coffee, maybe?" she asks cautiously.

"I don't know about that. I don't know if I can look at him right now. I don't know if I can go into that cafe."

"Sweetie, you are going to have to eventually see him. Especially if you are going to live in his neighborhood. You need to talk to him. Maybe after the appointment we can go to the cafe and you can talk to him. Tell him. He won't hate you. Tell him everything."

"I know you're probably right, Bren, I just don't know if it is something I can do yet. I will try. Okay? We can go get a coffee tomorrow, and if he is there, I can try and talk to him. Don't be surprised if you see me running out the door, though."

"As long as you try, that's all I can ask. I think he may surprise you. I've seen the way he looks at you. I really think he cares about you, and I think you need to let him in. Let yourself be open to him. He seems like a good guy from what you've told me."

"I will try. That is all I can give you right now. But now I have to try to find a job where someone will hire an eighteen-year-old pregnant girl."

"You will find something, even if I have to make my dad hire you," she says with a laugh.

I grab the laptop up again and start hunting for a job. This isn't going to be easy. I have never worked before, and I have no experience doing anything. I come across this ad for a store in the Old Port —it is an art gallery type store that also sells handmade jewelry. I write the information down and decide I want to apply in person. So, for the rest of the night, I have Bren help me prepare an outfit for tomorrow and figure out how to make myself look less like a zombie. Once we have taken care of that, we order in some Chinese food and lounge on the couch for the rest of the night. I have a feeling that tomorrow is going to be a good day and the start of my new life.

Bren and I arrive ten minutes early for the apartment appointment, but so does the landlord. He lets us into the building, and we walk up to the third floor. Not far from the stairwell, he stops at a door and opens it.

"Come on in," he says.

We walk past him, and I get a little thrill. It is a cute little place that has a raised section on one side big enough for a bed and then a little kitchenette on the other, with space in the middle. There is a door near the kitchenette that I assume is the bathroom. Opening the door, I find that I was right—there is a really nice bathroom with a walk-in closet off to one side. Bren follows me, and the look on her face is about as surprised as mine. The space is a lot nicer than I expected for the price.

"What do you think?" we hear from behind us.

Bren replies, "Well, it is nice and all, but I have a question. Do you have maybe another apartment with a bedroom? I think that I want to move with you, Kat. This place is nice, and if there is another one like it available, with maybe a bedroom attached or two, that would be even better."

"Well, we have a one-bedroom loft available. Same side of the building; just down this hall, actually."

"Can we take a look? How much for that one?"

"It is $750 a month. "

I pull Bren to the side and ask her what she is doing. Her parents will never let her move out of her house to live with me.

"Let's look at this place, and then I will call my mom. I am sure she will be okay with it."

"Okay. I guess we can look. It would be great to be with you, but if they say no, I will take the other place."

"Fine. Let's go."

We follow the landlord down the hall to the next apartment, and it is just as nice as the first place, but with a room added. It still has the raised area for a bed. We could put a curtain up to block it off from the rest of the apartment. *This could work, it could really work, and I wouldn't be alone.*

"If you would excuse me for a few minutes, I need to make a call," Bren says as she walks out the door to the hall.

I overhear her calling her mom and asking about the apartment. She seems to be okay with it. Bren enters back into the apartment a few minutes later with a smile on her face.

"Let's do this, K." She jumps up and down as she walks in to the apartment.

"Your mom said yes?"

"Well, sort of. She wants to see the place before we sign anything." Directing her words to the landlord, she says, "Can my mom see the place before we sign? She can be here in thirty minutes."

"That will work for me. I can go to the office and get the leasing paperwork and meet you ladies back here in thirty," he says.

"Okay, that sounds good to me," I reply.

We walk out of the apartment and out the front door to the building. This is the moment I realize just how close it is to James and his cafe. We will be four doors down, and the alley I was caught in by Trent is one building over. Once we hit the street, Bren turns and looks at me. "Coffee?"

I knew it was coming, but I didn't think it would come this soon. I sigh and nod.

"I suppose now is as good as any other time."

She links her arm with mine, and we walk down the street to the cafe. I have mixed emotions when I see Jayce behind the counter and no James in sight.

"Hey, ladies, your usual?" he asks with a smile on his face.

"Sounds good," I answer.

"Perfect," replies Bren.

"What are you ladies up to today?"

"Looking at an apartment. Four doors up the street. K and I are getting a place, since I will be staying local for college, and K is staying around here too."

"That sounds great. Are you going to take it?"

"Just waiting for my mother's approval, and then we will sign the lease. Hey, is James around? I have something I need to ask him," my sly friend asks.

"He is actually out of town for at least a week. He left me in charge until he gets back."

"Really? Where did he go off to?" I ask.

He shrugs. "I really don't know. He just said he had some things to deal with and that he would be back."

My heart sinks. As much as I feared talking to him, I miss him just as much. Bren looks over at me with a sad look and then her phone dings with a text message. Over her shoulder, I watch the conversation play out on the screen.

MOM: be there in 10
Bren: okay we're at The Java
MOM: See you there

"Let's go grab a seat and wait," Bren suggests.

We head over to the window so we can watch for her. She looks at me again with a sad expression.

"I'm sorry he isn't here. You can talk to him when he gets back."

"I know. I just realized that I actually miss him as much as I am scared to talk to him. I just don't know, Bren. What do I do? Who wants to be with a girl like me? Knocked up at eighteen and a stalker to boot."

"We will get everything figured out. Let's get this place, move in, and start a new life together. We'll have fun, we will stop the partying and drinking and everything, and just be us. I'll go to class, you go to work and bake that baby, and we will be awesome together."

"Do you know how much I love you? I couldn't do any of this without you." I wrap my arms around her in a tight hug then let go when I see her mom coming in the door. We both stand up to greet her.

"Hey, ladies, let's go look at this place you found. Oh, and Bren, thanks for saving Dad and me a few bucks by not living in the dorms. Your rent is nothing compared to room and board each semester." She winks at Bren.

We walk out the door and up the street to find Gary, the land-lord, waiting for us at the entrance.

"Hi. You must be Mom. The place is on the third floor. It's a walk up."

He opens the door and lets us go in front of him. Bren leads the way, and I hang in the back, taking my time. I have become a bit tired with all the running around we have done, and I still have to go to the gallery after this. Tina walks into the apartment and smiles. She seems to like the place. Then she asks the question I knew was coming.

"Where are you going to set the baby up?"

Bren replies, "I figured I would let K have the bedroom and then this elevated spot here I can put my bed and hang a curtain for privacy. If need be, we can share the closet or figure something out. This way, Kat has room for her and the baby in the bedroom."

This girl has thought of everything; she truly is my best friend. Her mom continues to take a look around the apartment and turns back around with a smile on her face.

"I like it. It is in a safe area, not to mention I know a certain guy down the street will be looking after you." She looks right at me, eyebrows raised.

"I don't know about that, but it would be nice."

"Kat, darling, everything will work out. I just know it. You ladies seem to have everything worked out. Now, Bren, you said rent was going to be $750 a month with all utilities included. Your room and board was going to be $900 a month, so why don't we just put the lease in our names, and then Dad and I will pay rent each month?"

I'm stunned. "Wait, what? It was my idea to get an apartment by myself and work for the rent. I can't live here and pay nothing. I need to pay for something."

Tina looks at me like I am crazy but concedes to letting me pay for cable and internet. She insists I need to save my money for the baby, especially since we don't know what will happen with my mom. Tina has taken me under her wing like I'm her own daughter, and I almost want to cry. Now I am certain I am starting to feel loved and wanted.

Gary gets the paperwork together and lays it on the counter for Tina to sign. I feel weird letting them do this, but apparently, I have no choice in the matter at this point. Bren's mom writes a check and gives it to Gary then he hands the keys to her.

"Welcome home, ladies!" she says as she jumps up and down with her daughter. I can't help but laugh—I now know where Bren gets it from.

We lock up and make our way to the street. We part ways with plans to meet up at the house later and decide what Bren needs to take with her to the apartment. Tomorrow, we will start to move in.

Bren walks me down to the gallery, checking to make sure I still look good, and sends me in the door with a hug. This place is beautiful. The artwork on the walls is so full of color, and the jewelry in the cases is amazing. I go to the counter and find a very slim lady with bright-green eyes and blonde hair. When I approach the counter, she greets me.

"Hello there, can I help you with anything?"

"Hi, yes, my name is Katarina. I saw that you had an ad for an assistant here in the gallery? I wanted to come in personally rather than apply online."

She takes my hand and shakes it. "Ah, yes, my name is Gloria. Tell me about yourself."

What do I say? How much do I tell her? I'll never get this job.

"I just graduated from high school, and I am about to move into an apartment a few doors down. I have decided to take some time to myself and not go to college in the fall. So, I am looking for a job where I can learn and experience something new. These pieces on the walls are amazing, by the way."

"Why, thank you. I like to look for new artists who need a chance to be seen. These are actually done by students from the college here in Portland. So, Katarina, you seem excited and full of energy. I like that. How about we try you out for a week? See if this is something that you want to do. Then we can talk about a more permanent position for you then."

"That would be amazing, Gloria. When do you want me to start?"

"Let's have you come in on Monday. You said you were moving, so get yourself settled this weekend, and I will see you Monday morning at nine."

"Thank you so much." I shake her hand again and head toward the door. I turn and wave bye to her and say, "See you on Monday."

I meet Bren back at the car and fling my arms around her, jumping us both up and down. She is starting to rub off on me. "I start Monday! But it is a trial. She said we will talk more the next Monday to see if we are a good fit together."

"Yay! I am so excited for you. See, I told you this was going to be a good day for you. Now it is a good day for the both of us. Let's head back to my house and start packing."

We get in her car and head to her house. This has been a great day, but I still miss James. I sit in the passenger seat and wonder where he ran off to without even a text to me. Maybe he decided to believe me when I said I didn't want to be with him.

James

I land in New York, and as I get to baggage claim to grab my bag, I get a call. Looking at the caller ID, I see that it's Grant my private investigator.

"Hey, what's going on?

"I just got some intel about his location. He appears to be having dinner at the Rocking Horse Bistro tonight at seven. I'm about to text you a picture of him so you know who to look for. It is hard to get into the restaurant, but there is a bar area, so maybe you can go and grab a drink while you look for him."

"Thanks, man. I just landed in New York. Stay in touch."

I grab my bag and head out the door and hail a cab. I have a room reserved at the Riverside Hotel. While I am in the cab, I look up the Rocking Horse Bistro to see where it is located. Luckily, it is only two blocks away from the hotel. Once I am checked in, it is getting close to the time I need to leave. I take a quick shower and dress in my best suit and walk out the door. I don't bother to hail a cab since it's so close. When I get to the Rocking Horse Bistro, I go straight to the bar. I didn't even bother to try and make a reservation. Once I get a seat at the bar, I take another look at the picture that Grant sent me. When I look up, I see him walking in the door. He looks like me, and I don't like that one bit. I sit and watch him from my seat at the bar as I drink my scotch. He is sitting with a beautiful woman I don't recognize. It looks like they are on a date.

I wait until she gets up to use the restroom and approach him.

I don't say a word as I take the seat that was just vacated, and he looks at me like he's seen a ghost. Yeah, I was right. We could be twins.

"Who are you?"

"Apparently, I am your brother. We share the same asshole father."

"What do you want? I know who my father is, and I want nothing to do with him."

"You may think differently once you hear what I have to say. Meet me tomorrow at the Riverside Hotel at eleven, and I will explain everything to you. I know you want me gone before she comes back, so just meet me, okay?"

"I have to admit, I'm curious, so I'll meet you. I will see you tomorrow at eleven. We can grab some brunch in the restaurant."

"See you then." I disappear as his date starts back toward the table. I go back to the hotel and up to my room, where I order room service, change my clothes, and relax for the night. I made contact, now I just need to convince him he needs to take over the Family instead of me.

I wake up the next morning, shower, and order room service for some coffee and a muffin then make some calls.

"Hey, Jayce, how did it go this morning?"

"Everything went well, boss. We are open and running smoothly. I did what you said and left two hundred in the drawer and put the rest in the safe."

"Thanks, Jayce, you are doing great. I will call you tonight and see how the day went."

"Sounds good to me. Talk to you later."

Once I am done checking in with Jayce, I call Grant.

"Hey, it's me. I made contact. The guy looked like he saw a ghost when he saw me. I guess no one told him I exist. We are meeting at eleven."

"Good to hear, let me know if you need anything else."

"I will. Thanks again for all the help."

My calls are made, my coffee has been consumed, and now I have some time to myself. I don't want to go into my head, but I do. Kat is sitting in the front of my mind all the time. If only she would text me, call me, something to let me know she is all right. With my phone in my hand, I open my messages and debate texting her, but decide to keep my distance for the moment and get this situation taken care of. I need to keep her safe. The time is getting close to my meeting, so I decide to go downstairs a little early and get a table in the corner away from everyone else in the restaurant. Before I know it, it's eleven, and he is walking toward me.

He sits down, and the first words out of his mouth are, "Talk. I don't have a lot of time on my hands."

"This won't take long, I hope. Question, do you really know who our dad is?"

"I thought I knew who my dad was, but now I'm not so sure. My father is a businessman, and my mom worked as a waitress up until she became pregnant with me. His name is Joe. He left us when I was a kid. He's not worth my time."

"I hate to break it to you this way, but Joe is not your father. Our biological father is Al Milano, the leader of the Boston Milano's. He is dying and wants me to take over. He said that there was no one else to do it. I didn't believe him, so I went looking. I found you. "

He looks skeptical. "Al Milano is our father? How do you know this?"

"You know that place your mom waitressed at, the strip club in Boston? Well, so did my mom, and it's owned by the Milano's. My mother was married, too. Apparently, good old' dad wanted our mothers and he got them, but I am not sure if he knows about you. From what I was able to tell, you are three years older than me. I don't want this. I have a good, clean life in Portland. I was wondering if leading the Family would be of interest to you. Maybe you could bring your Uncle Jacob with you. Did you know he is married to Al's sister?"

"Are you serious? You want me to stroll into the office of Al Milano, introduce myself as his son, and take over when he dies in a few weeks?"

"That is exactly what I want you to do. I want nothing to do with this. Hell, I don't even care if we ever talk again. I just want my life to go back the way it was before he found me."

"I am going to have to talk to my uncle about all this. To be the lead and not a lackey would be a step up in life, but I would have to handle things carefully here. From my understanding, there is no current bad blood between us. How long are you staying?"

"As long as it takes. I need you to go to Boston with me."

This is actually going better than I had planned, but when you have a twenty-five-year-old lackey who is already involved with the mob, I didn't expect it to be a hard sell. This is a major step up in their game of life.

We eat our food and make small talk, getting a few minor details about each other, then we go our separate ways.

"I'll be in touch."

I go back to my room and make a call.

"I'll be there in person, on my terms, by the end of the week."

I don't wait for a reply; I just hang up the phone.

Chapter Twenty-One

Katarina

It has been almost a week since I have heard from James. He last texted me on Sunday, and here it is Thursday and nothing, he's been gone since Monday. Jayce still doesn't know when he will be back, so I finally break down and send him a text.

K: Hope you are okay. I need to talk to you.

I impatiently wait for a text back and don't get one. Bren and I are packing everything that she will need in the apartment. Truthfully, it's mostly clothes that are coming with us. I just have a couple duffle bags, so my part is easy until I get my things from mom's house. Now we just have to figure out what we are going to do about furniture. It's a good thing we waited a few days before doing anything with the apartment. We load up Bren's car with as much as we can and drive over to the apartment. I arranged for the cable and internet to be hooked up today. I was shocked that they had an appointment this afternoon. I have to be there for the waiting period. Got to love sitting and waiting for four hours when they almost always show up at the very last minute of the time block.

Bren brought a couple of pillows with her, so once we lug up our suitcases and she runs back down for the last few things, we sit. Looking around the place, I start making a list of everything we are going to need. It's kind of exciting, starting fresh.

"Hey, Bren, here is my list." I read off the list to her. "Can you think of anything else we will need right away? Your mom said you can take the TV in your room, right?"

"Yeah, she did. What about sheets and towels? And where are we going to find a couch? Do you want to look at the secondhand store down the street?"

"I'll stay here; you can go look. I have to wait for the cable guy."

Bren gets up off the floor and grabs her purse. "Okay. I'll send you pictures if I find anything good." She walks out the door, and I am left to my thoughts in my head.

I'm worried that James gave up on me when I ignored him.

I'm worried that Trent will find me again.

I'm worried that my life is too messed up for anyone to want me like that, and if my life is too messed up for another person, what business do I have bringing a baby into it?

Luckily, I have Bren and Tina on my side. I wish my mother believed in me the way Tina does. She wants me to talk to my mom when she gets back this weekend from her honeymoon, to tell her everything. I know I should, but I just don't know. Maybe if I have Bren and Tina bring me to the house, I can do it with them on my side. Actually, I know I can. I shoot off a text to mom.

Kat: we need to talk when you get home. I have some things to tell you.

MOM: I know we do.

MOM: be back Sunday early afternoon. I will text when we arrive.

MOM: You can come to the new house after.
Kat: Okay

I then text Tina.

Kat: Tina are you busy Sunday evening?
Tina: No. What do you need?
Kat: Can you go with me to my mom's?
Tina: Sure sweetie. Let me know the time.
Kat: She will text when she gets home.
Tina: Sounds good

As I'm putting my phone on the charger, the door buzzes. I like how this building has the old-school door buzzer and speaker.

I push the button to talk. "Hello?"

"I'm here to install the cable and internet," the guy on the other end replies.

I buzz him in and realize he is actually here at the beginning of the time slot window. That never happens. I hear a knock at the door and absently open the door, shocked to see a guy in a very expensive black suit.

Hesitantly, I ask, "I'm guessing you're not the cable guy?"

"Ma'am," he says, "I am here to give you a gift from my boss."

He hands me an envelope with a note inside, written on fancy cardstock.

Take this gift and enjoy!
Now stay away from my son.
He needs to stay in Boston.
You don't want to know what I can do if you don't.
-Al

Behind the notecard was a check for $25,000. As I get done

reading the note, I look up, and the guy in the suit is gone. I close the door and slide down until my butt hits. *What am I going to do with this, and who is he talking about? I don't want this check. And who is Al?*

I don't know how long I sit there, staring at the check, but I soon snap out of it and put the card and check in the envelope and then drop it on the counter by my purse. I can't tell anyone about this. Not yet. The buzzer goes off again, and I realize I now kind of hate it. I answer again with a sharper "Hello?"

"Ma'am, this is Carlos from Coastal Cable. I am here to install your cable and internet today."

I buzz him up, and this time I make sure the door chain is on before I open the door when he knocks. Fool me once and all that. He shows me his ID, and once I verify he is who he says he is, I unlatch the chain and let him in.

"Hi, thanks for showing me some ID. Come on in."

"Good afternoon, ma'am. I'm here to hook up the cable and internet. Do you have a TV set up yet?"

"No, we haven't brought it over yet, but we want to put it here." I show him where we will have the TV, and he gets everything set up, so we just have to plug it in and hook the cable to it and we are good. The internet gets set up too, and he is off with a quick signature on his sheet.

Bren comes back a little while later with a disappointed look on her face, so I make a suggestion to her.

"I assume with the look on your face that they didn't have anything. Mom gets back on Sunday, and your mom is going over with me to talk to her. I want you to come too, but I was thinking that since she is moving out of the house, I can ask her if we can grab some of the furniture she isn't going to be using. What do you think?"

"First off, I am glad that you are going to talk to her, and, yes, I will go with you. Second, I think that is a good idea. Better than her having to put stuff into storage. Did the guy come by and hook up the cable?"

"Yeah, he just left a little while ago."

Bren walks over to the kitchen counter and notices the envelope sitting there that I forgot to put in my purse. "What is this?"

"Nothing important." I shove it in my purse. "What are we doing for dinner?"

"I think we should head back over to my house. Mom and Dad are grilling. We need to get as much homemade food as possible before we have to fend for ourselves."

I laugh and say, "Sounds good to me." I look at my phone and check for like the thousandth time for a reply text. No such luck. We both grab our purses and head for the door.

"Let's go grab some coffee before we head to your house. By the way, we need to figure out a bed situation fast. I don't care if we have to use an air mattress. Did your mom say anything about the furniture in your room?"

"I honestly haven't even asked. This whole thing kinda happened a little fast. But I am so excited to live with you, Kat. This is going to be so fun."

We head over to The Java to grab a coffee before we get into her car. As we walk in, I look around to see if James is back. He isn't. "Hey, Jayce, when is the boss man coming back?"

"Hey. Still haven't heard from him about when he'll be home. He said about a week, and he took off on Monday. I assume he won't be back until Sunday or Monday. "

"How goes being the boss?" Bren asks.

I look at her and notice that there is something different in her eyes when she looks at him. I think she is starting to like him more than as a friend. Interesting.

"Not as bad as I was expecting. The schedule got worked out before James left, and I don't have to do the books or anything. I just unlock the door in the morning and lock it at night and during the day make sure everyone is doing what they are supposed to be doing. What kills me is getting up so damn early to be here to open. Most days I go home and take a nap before coming back."

"I don't blame ya. I would do the same if I were you," Bren says to him. Now I notice a little bit of flirting. Jayce makes our regular coffee drinks and hands them to us.

"Thanks, Jayce. We need to get going to Bren's house for dinner. We have to grab as many free meals as we can before we are fending for ourselves up the street. See you later."

"Bye, Jayce, see you soon," Bren adds as we walk out the door.

As we walk up the street I look over to Bren and waggle my brows. "Jayce?"

"No idea what you are talking about," she says with a smirk on her face.

"Hey, he is a nice guy. I know he wasn't trying to give me a hard time at prom. It was just way too much, under the circumstances. I've still gotta figure out what's going on with James—if the guy would text me back or something."

"You texted him? When?"

"This morning after you left; he hasn't replied. I don't know if he is busy or ignoring me, but I know I need to talk to him. I know I need to tell him what happened and how I became pregnant. Maybe he would understand things better if I explained. I just wish I knew what he was doing, what the emergency was, and if he is okay. James doesn't seem like the type to just get up and go like he did."

"I agree with you; it isn't like him. I'm sure he is okay. He will be back soon. Then you can talk to him and tell him everything. Release the secrets."

"I know you're right, but I'm scared. What if he looks at me differently? Doesn't want anything to do with me anymore?"

"The way that man treats you and looks at you, I don't think he would run away screaming. I kinda think he would be more the type to fight your battles for you. He is protective of you, Kat. I don't know why, but he is. I saw his reaction when you went somewhere with Jayce. That man has the tightest jaw and quickly makes an escape. I think he would rather leave than beat someone's face in, especially his manager."

"I've seen it too. Believe me, I've seen it. I just don't get it, though. I'm nothing special, and he hardly knows me."

"He knows enough about you to know he wants you. Heck, he waited until you were eighteen to touch you. He wants to do things right. It will all be okay."

We get to her house and make our way toward the backyard, where we find her parents by the grill.

"Hey, can we join you?"

"Trying to get some home cooking before you are out on your own? Oh, and we were expecting you both for dinner," her mom says

I pull Bren off to the side to ask her, "Has anyone told your father?"

"Look at him, do you think he knows anything?" Bren laughs.

"I am serious, Bren. Has your mom told him about my situation?"

"I don't think so. If she had, I do believe he would be acting much differently. He thinks of you like a daughter too, ya know. I am sure he would be loading up a shotgun in search of Trent if he knew the truth."

"Oh, um, okay. Can we not tell him yet? At least, wait until my mom knows. Before long, I may just have to send out a memo and get it over with," I joke, but Bren doesn't laugh and looks at me with narrowed eyes. "I know it isn't funny. I just went from not telling anyone—including my best friend—to making a list of everyone I have to tell. It isn't something that's easy to do. I just sometimes have to joke to release some of my stress. I'm sorry."

"No, I am sorry. I know you have a lot going on in that head. Everything has kind of exploded around you this past week. As long as you know I am here and don't keep secrets from me again, we will be all set. I got you."

At that moment, I feel guilty about not telling her about the guy in the black suit and the card with that huge check. I need to get through dinner, and then when we are alone later, I will tell her. I have to tell her, because I need her friendship. I need her in my life.

Dinner is great, and her mom and dad go out to the garage after we eat and grab us some air mattresses. Then her mom throws some sheets and pillows at us and sends us on our way back to our own place. As I sit in the car, I make a promise to myself: I will not keep secrets from Bren. Once we get our beds set up and the TV hooked up, we sit and relax. After we're settled, I spill my guts.

"Bren, I have to tell you something. I lied to you earlier about that card on the counter. It is something." I pull out the envelope I grabbed earlier and hand it to her. She opens it, and her eyes go wide.

"What the hell is this? And god*damn* that is a lot of money."

"I buzzed up what I thought was the cable guy earlier, after you left, and it wasn't him. It was a guy in a black suit. He didn't say much but handed me the card. After I read it and looked up, he was gone. I have no idea what this is about, but it scares me. Someone with a lot of money wants me to stay away from someone. It's not like I have a lot of people in my life. The only one I can think this is about is James. This makes me even more scared for what is going on with him."

Bren wraps her arms around me and soothes me by saying, "It will all be okay. I am here for you. We will get this all figured out. What are you going to do with the check?"

"I don't know."

James

I wake up the next morning to a knock on the door. I open it to find Jackson on the other side, flanked by two guys, all three dressed in suits.

"Who are the goons?" I ask as I open the door for them to walk in. Jackson and one of the guys steps inside, but the other turns around to stand guard outside the door.

"My security team. Now, let's get down to business. "

"Um, can you give me a minute to throw some clothes on and order some coffee? I wasn't expecting you so soon."

"You get dressed, and I will get the coffee up here. Then we will talk."

I go into the bedroom of my suite and put on a pair of jeans and a T-shirt then run into the bathroom to brush my teeth and hair. When I am all cleaned up, I go back out to the living area, where the coffee is just being brought in.

"That was fast. Let me get a cup, and then we can sit and talk about all this."

I grab my cup and pour in a bunch of sugar and cream—because nothing tastes as good as my coffee at the cafe, but I need the caffeine—and go sit on the couch opposite Jackson.

"So, what do you think about what I said? Did you talk to your uncle about it at all?"

"Yeah, he confirmed what you said about my aunt, as much as it seems a little bit too close to home by having my mom hook up with my aunt's brother. He told me it was all true. What I don't understand is why all the secrets? Why nobody ever thought I should know."

"I feel you there. I didn't find out until my mom and dad both died at the same time in a car accident. Al came out of the woodwork and has been trying to get me involved with the family ever since. I have resisted up to now. This time, I am desperate. I asked him about someone else taking over instead of me, and I caught a look in his eye right before he said there was no one. I knew in that second that there was, and I went looking. Apparently, you aren't hard to trace back to him and were easy to find with the right P.I."

"Well, good to know I am traceable. Not really, but thanks for the heads up. I have to admit I was a bit shocked when you approached the table. I saw myself looking back at me. It is nice to know I have a brother. So, tell me about you, and why you don't want in."

"I live in Portland, Maine; my parents weren't great, but they were my parents. I'm twenty-two and was seventeen, almost eighteen when they took too many drugs and ran off the road effectively killing them. I am now cleaned up, no more drugs for me, and I own a building in the Old Port with a coffee shop store front. I like my life the way it is, and I don't want in. I just found out last week that he has his eye on a girl I'm interested in. He's somehow involved with a guy who knocked her around in an alley by my building. I found her after he was gone, and we ended up in the ER that night. I don't know why he wants me so badly, when there is you that fits into the family way of life so much better. I realize he's dying, but I don't know him other than all the bad he has put into my life, and I'm not interested in knowing."

"I see where you are coming from, but I think I know why he doesn't want me. My uncle tried to combine the families when he married your aunt. Al didn't want any part of it, to the point he disowned his sister. He has so much shit on her that she stayed away and convinced my uncle to stay away too. I bet that he wants me to stay hidden as the next in line so that the families stay separated. My uncle isn't a lackey in this family. He's at the table with all the other family members high in ranks. If I go with you to Boston and he comes with me, we will have a joined, two-territory family. I will make sure of that. We are too closely linked."

"You are the next in line, since you are older than me. Even if I play his game and he dies in a few weeks I will bring you in to take over. If you want it, I will walk away. I have one week from today to pack my stuff and go to Boston to take over, or he says he will destroy Kat more than he already has. I would rather we go together, and you take over and I go home to Kat. What do you think of showing up at his office?"

"Maybe the shock of my presence will kill him on the spot?" he says as he gets up and walks to the window. Speaking to the window, he continues. "It's Thursday now, so let me tie some loose threads, and then tomorrow night we can head toward Boston. Saturday, we can go surprise dear old dad."

I let out the breath I am holding as relief washes over me. "That sounds like a plan. I don't know how it will go, but either way, we have a backup plan. Either way, he will know I know one of his secrets, and now you do too."

Jackson leaves me his phone number in my phone and shoots off a text to himself, so he has mine. We agree to meet up at four and drive up to Boston with his security team.

I haven't been to New York in a long time, so I decide to spend the rest of my day wandering around the city. When I walk by Tiffany's, the blue calls my name. I walk into the store and look around for something that screams out Katarina. I want to show her in some way what she means to me. I decide on a delicate rose gold chain bracelet with a small diamond. I have them box it up and hand over my card to pay for it. Once I sign, I am presented with a small blue bag tied with a bow.

This bracelet reminds me of Kat. She is delicate and has a ray of light that bursts my heart. The diamond is her ray of light, small enough just for me to see. As I walk out of the store, my mind goes directly to her, and I can't get her out of my head. I look at my phone to see what time it is and realize I have a message waiting for me. I take a look and realize that she reached out to me. She sent a text to me this morning. It must have been when Jackson was putting his info into my phone and texting himself. All it said was, "Hope you are okay. We need to talk." I let it sit there for the rest of the day without a reply. I want to talk to her, but right now I just want to keep her safe, and I need to deal with my father first. Later that night, as I sit in my room, still not able to get her out of my head, I send her a text.

J: I'm okay. Talk when I get back.

I don't get a reply, but I didn't figure I would since it is so late.

I wake up the next morning after actually getting a full night's sleep, and I call down to room service for some breakfast. Once it arrives, I sit and eat in a silence that is too much to bear, then shower and put myself together for the day. I pack my bags and head out the door with still a few hours to go until I am due to meet Jackson. I decide to leave my bag with the concierge desk and head out to Central Park across the street. I just wander around, hoping that this day goes as planned and that I can go back to living the life I made for myself.

As usual, my mind goes back to her. To the way that she looked laying on the ground of that alley. To her waking up and screaming in pain. To her scared face as she told me she was pregnant. I want to take care of her. I want to be there for her, and I want to protect her. So far, all I have done is fail her. It is my fault that she was attacked in that alley, and I will never forgive myself for bringing that on her.

Before I know it, the alarm on my phone goes off to let me know I need to head back to the hotel to meet Jackson. Once I arrive, I grab my bag and go to the lounge for a drink. Who says you have to wait until five o'clock? I get two fingers of scotch and wait for their arrival.

Jackson soon enters the room and heads straight for me.

"We need to talk before we go. I just got word that Al had one of his guys drop off a note to Kat at her new apartment, with a threat and a $25,000 check enclosed. He wants to pay her to stay away from you. Do you think she will take the money or rip it apart? Is this all worth it for a girl?"

"This is more than for a girl, Jackson. Even if there was no girl, I don't want that life. I want *my* life. Did you say her *new* apartment? And how did you know who I was talking about?"

"Looks like her friend Bren and her mom signed a lease this week, and the girls are living there together. That is all I know. I did my own digging. You are easy to find things out about too. I have someone looking out for her, especially since she is pregnant. Is the baby yours? You don't have to worry that is the last time she will be approached."

"We need to get this done so I can get back and take care of what's mine. I wish the baby was mine but I'm not that lucky. She has no idea about any of this. Let's go," I grind out.

"Okay, man, I just wanted you to be sure this is what you want to do. Also, I wanted you to know what he was up to. I give you props for being able to stay away from it as long as you have. Let's get you and your girl out of this mess."

We head out the door to the waiting SUV, and I toss my bag in the back and get in. We are off to Boston. No one seems to be in the mood to talk, so it is a long, quiet ride. I actually haven't heard his security team say a word since I met them. I check my phone to see if Kat has replied and she has, just one word.

K<3: Okay

I decide, after what I was told, that I need to check on her.

J: Are you okay?
K<3: I'm good. Come back soon.

I want to pick the phone up so bad and hear her voice, but I don't. I sit there in silence as we drive down I-95 toward Boston. A few hours later, we pull up to the Grand Empire Hotel. I grab my bag and follow Jackson into the hotel. This place is amazing. I may have to bring Kat here some weekend.

We check into a three-bedroom suite and form a plan for the morning. A call to room service takes care of dinner, and once it arrives, we eat and continue to plan. It is a really simple plan. I walk in flanked by my new security team of three, I go to my father's office or bedroom or wherever his sick body lies, and we confront him. Jackson reveals himself, and that is when we plan for all hell to break loose.

Right when we think we are done for the night, I get a call.

"James, I know you are in Boston. Get your ass to your dad's house now. He won't make it through the night, the nurse says. We need you here now," his number one goon calls to tell me.

"Well, Jackson, are you ready for a late night? Looks like Dad is worse off than he said. My presence has been requested *now*."

We set the plan in motion, with Jackson dressed in a dark suit like his team. He has the added fedora to cover his dark blonde hair and his face a little bit, since we could pass as twins.

We drive over to his place on Beacon Hill and find a place to park not too far away, surprisingly. One guy stays with the car, and the other comes with Jackson and me to the door. I don't even need to ring the bell because it is opening for me as I walk up. I acknowledge the guy with a nod and walk through the door with Jackson and his team member on my heels.

"Who do you have here?" asks the man at the door.

"If I am taking over this show, I need my own security team. Where is the old man, anyway?"

He replies, "In his room, but only you go, not them."

"From the sounds of it, I will be your boss by morning, so I take whoever I want with me." I head toward his room on the second floor and leave Jackson's team member at the top of the stairs with a view of both the entry and my father's bedroom door. Jackson and I walk into the room and see that he is in really bad shape. I ask the nurse if he is lucid, and she says he is. He knows what is going on around him, but his lungs are quickly shutting down. He is basically drowning from the inside out. She says they have been waiting for my arrival before giving him morphine so that he would still be lucid when I got here.

I walk over to the man dying in the bed. I don't know him, nor do I feel any pity for him. He was just a man I wanted out of my life.

His death meant I was finally going to get my wish. I am finally going to be free.

"I'm here."

"You came. Now you can take over the family. Now—" He pauses to cough and attempts to take a deep breath but coughs again. He starts over. "Now your girl will be safe. I can die at peace, knowing there's someone here to protect the family."

"I'm not going to lead the family, Dad, my brother is."

His eyes widen as I speak the words. He thinks I am bluffing. Then over walks Jackson, taking off his hat to reveal himself. My dad's eyes widen even bigger, and he coughs as he tries to take a breath.

"Who...who told you about him? Why is he here? It is you who will lead, James, not that POS. He is not Milano; he is part of the Castillo family. Blood or no blood, he will not lead."

"Nice to see you too, Dad," Jackson says to him. "No one told him about me, he found me on his own. He so desperately wants away from you that he went looking for another option. That has to tell you something, Dad," he says with disdain in his voice.

Al tries to push him away. "Go to hell, boy. Leave a dying man in peace."

I explain. "We are here to tell you how it is going to happen. You're past the point of arguing. You die tonight, and I will lead for about five seconds—long enough to appoint Jackson as the new head of family. No matter how you look at it, I am out within the next twenty-four hours."

"You will ruin this family. The Milano and Castillo families do not need to mix. I will not allow it," he forces out with another cough to follow, struggling and failing to sit up.

"I am so glad you are supportive of me and that you love me as much as I love you," Jackson says. "It was nice to see you, but I think I must be off. I have plans to make for moving into this house. James, are you coming, or are we going to stick around and wait for the old man to die?"

There is no love in this room between us. I can see my brother and I becoming close eventually, but right now we have a job to do. I walk over to my dad, kiss his forehead, and tell him to rest in peace.

"Since you are this sick and not in any condition to lead the family, I am taking over right this second. I will get everyone together downstairs and fill them in on what will be happening. I will also let the nurse in here to finally give you that dose of morphine so that you can maybe die in peace tonight. You wanted a mean alpha from me? You just got him. I am in charge of this now, and you and your lackeys can go to hell. You know that check will never clear the bank, right, old man? She is stronger than you think she is."

"If you don't take over, I have one of my guys on standby in Portland. Someone in this house respects me enough to follow directions, so the second you hand the reins over to him is the second she goes away for good."

Both my brother and I turn toward him, fury burning in our eyes. I can't help it, I lie to the old man, just to save her life. I look over to

Jackson, hoping that he will follow along with me, grasp that this is a lie. He knows the card I am about to play, because like he said earlier, he has done his research, he knows she is pregnant. He knows what I am about to do to save her life.

"So, you would kill your grandchild, because you want me as head that bad? You remove her from the picture, you remove my child—your grandchild, your own blood—from the picture too."

A look of shock crosses his face. He doesn't know what to do with this information; I can tell by the look in his eyes. He has Jackson call the nurse in so he can request the presence of one of his guys from downstairs. That is the second I know he has made his decision. My lie worked in my favor—he believed me. And now I will become free of him.

"I have one request from you, please stay here, if not in this room this house. I would prefer you stay in here until I am gone," he asks both of us. We both nod our heads and find a seat in the room.

When Al's guy comes into the room, he doesn't see us in the shadows. "Do I make the call?"

"No, the hit is called off. She carries my grandchild. I want you to know I free James of the head of family title and give it willingly to Jackson. Once I am gone, my eldest son will be leading the family, as it should be."

Jackson and I stand up from the shadows and into the light where he can see us. He didn't know there was another son, I can tell by the look in his eyes.

"So, you were the one that was going to call the hit on my girl. Good to know," I say and go back into the shadows. "I think you better call your guy off the girl now, right here. If you don't want to, I have my own guy on her who would gladly take yours out. He isn't very good at staying hidden by the way. Let me guess, Trent?"

The call is made, and he leaves. Jackson told me that he was keeping his guy on her anyway, so she'll be safe until I can see to her myself. The nurse comes in and gives the dose of morphine to our old man, and Jackson and I sit in the room in silence listening to the machines and monitors. About two or three hours go by—it is either really late at night or early in the morning however you want to see it—when the machines go off. There is no more beep–beep–beep. There is just a constant beeeeeeeeeeeeeeeeeeeeeeeep and a flat line across the heart monitor. He's gone, and I'm free.

The nurse does her thing, disconnecting the machines and monitors, and Jackson and I walk silently from the room. We promise to stay in touch, and I promise him if I need anything, I will let him know. His first security team member motions me to get in the car and brings me down the street where there is a car waiting for me in a parking lot. I get out and grab my bag and head toward the car with One, as I call him. The trunk opens, and I put my bag in, close the trunk, and get in the back seat.

"Welcome, Mr. James, I should have you in Portland, depending on traffic, in a little under two hours."

I sit back and close my eyes, ready to get my girl.

Chapter Twenty-Two

Katarina

We wake up Friday morning and get ourselves ready for the day. I have an appointment at Planned Parenthood today for my first official ultrasound, and I am excited. At this appointment, they are going to check me over, do an ultrasound, and refer me out to a prenatal care clinic and go over what I need to do to get myself set up with the state medical program.

"You know, Bren, I am still on my mother's insurance. Maybe after this appointment I should go back to my own OB-GYN. Get better care than state insurance. What do you think?"

"I think that's a good idea, but I would get all the information today and talk to your mom Sunday night about it. See where she is after you tell her the truth."

"See, this is why you are my best friend; you always know what to do. Are you excited to see the baby today? I sure am. I want to make sure everything is still okay and see the little bean wiggle around."

"I'm so excited. I can't wait to be Auntie Bren."

Bren parks the car, and we head to the door to be buzzed in. I get signed in and then we wait.

"We should go to Target after this appointment and look at some curtains. We need to start putting the place together."

"We should. I most definitely need to find something that will go with the apartment and my hidey area. This will be a fun day. We need a fun day with no issues."

A nurse comes through the door and calls my name. "Here we go!" I do the normal height, weight, and vitals, and then get sent to the restroom for a urine sample. *How fun.* Once I get back into the room, the nurse is waiting for me along with the insurance counselor.

"Hi, Kat. I'm Nancy, and I am going to go over a few things with you real fast before you get on with your checkup. So, I understand that you have insurance under your mom, but now that you are eighteen you are eligible to be covered through the state. It is a bit of a process, but I am here to walk you through it. I am going to give you a packet for you to fill out and then you need to take it to the office downtown. They will decide there if you are eligible. In the meantime, we need to refer you to the prenatal clinic for the rest of your care. Are you okay with all of this?"

"Yes, I understand. It isn't an automatic thing, and I may be denied. I was actually thinking of asking my mom this weekend about keeping me on her policy. Until then, I will take the information and move forward. Thank you so much, Nancy."

"If you have any questions, here is my card, just give me a call. Have a great day, ladies."

Nancy walks out the door, and Mary the nurse comes over to me to start asking questions.

"So, Kat, have you had any problems since your last visit we need to be aware of?"

"Yes, actually. I was in the ER last Saturday night for severe pain because of an assault. I was kicked in the stomach. The ER doctor said to stay off my feet as much as I can but that everything looked good in the ultrasound that they did."

Mary notates my file with the information then walks over to me on the table and asks for me to lie down. She takes a tape measure and after feeling around my stomach, measures my belly with it. "Looks like your uterus is measuring just fine, twelve weeks. Let's move on to the ultrasound." She gets the machine up and running and moves it toward me. I look over toward Bren, who has a huge smile on her face.

"A little bit excited, are we?" I ask her. She looks like she is about to burst and is trying to not do her signature jumping up and down.

"Uh, yeah, just a little bit," she replies.

Mary puts the cold gel on my stomach and has a look of apology as I suck in a little breath. She grabs her wand and starts moving it across my skin. She turns the volume up, and we hear the strong heartbeat. Once again, I get tears in my eyes but brush them away. When I look at the screen, I see the little bean moving around, but then I notice the nurse's face. She looks a little concerned. Before I know it, she is excusing herself to go speak with the doctor.

"Oh, my God, Bren, what if something's wrong," I whisper as new tears hit my eyes. Bren takes a strong hold of my hand and squeezes. She doesn't say anything; we just sit in silence and wait for the doctor to come in and take a look at the screen herself.

"Hi, Kat, nice to see you again. Let me take a look and see what we have here."

"Is something wrong?" I ask.

"I'm going to take a look and find out. Mary thought she saw something but wanted me to take a look and verify." She moves the wand around on my skin some more then stops in one area. "Kat, it looks like there is a small tear in the placenta. Everything else looks good with the baby. I understand you had an incident the other night. This may be a result of that but was probably not noticeable then."

"What do I need to do to fix it? Tell me, I will do it," I rush out when she seems like she is done talking.

"Well, what I need you to do is to go on bedrest for the next four to six weeks. You can get up to shower and use the restroom and walk around the house, but just to go from one room to the other. I want you to stay put as much as possible. Catch up on any shows you have missed lately or read a few books. Right now, we need to keep you as low-key as possible. Can you do that?"

Bren rushes to answer, "Yes, she will do that, I will make sure she does."

"I want you to follow up with your OB-GYN you choose to go to from this point on in about two weeks. I hope that if we keep you low-key it will repair on its own. Other than that, the baby looks great. Per the ultrasound, we have you at eleven weeks and three days, so we were right with the due date. I am going to leave Mary with you, and she is going to take some measurements and pictures for you to take home. Please don't worry. Everything will be okay as long as you follow directions." She walks out the door, and Mary goes about her measurements.

"Well, I guess that job I got is now out of the question," I say to Bren sadly. "And the trip to Target."

Mary finishes up, wipes me off, and hands me a stack of photos. I thank her, and we head out the door to go back home to sit and wait for the next few weeks to pass by.

As we are driving home, I sit and look at all the new pictures I have. *Do I have a little girl or a little boy growing inside me?* When we get back to our street, Bren drops me off right at the door to the building. She yells instructions of not to move and then goes to park her car. Before I know it, Bren is at my side, grabbing my arm and treating me as if I can't walk. I shrug loose of her grip and tell her I can walk on my own, and I do—up three flights of stairs. Which is probably not what the doctor had in mind about taking it easy.

Panting a little as we walk in the door of our apartment, I realize

I've got no place to sit but the air mattress, which looks a little saggy after a night of sleeping. "You know, Bren, it would be a very good time to have a couch in here." We both laugh, but the thought makes me worry.

If my life wasn't hard enough, I have an apartment I need to furnish, and I can't go anywhere to get it done. I decide it's a good time to take a nap. As I get as comfortable as I can on the air mattress, I hear Bren on the phone with her mom.

"She has nowhere to relax and sit, we need a couch, a futon, we need *something*." And then I hear nothing—her mom must be talking. "That sounds great, Mom. We are going to ask her mom on Sunday if they have anything we can use." Another pause of silence. "See you then, love you." Bren comes back in the room and says, "We have that futon in the garage; my dad will bring it over after work today."

"Sounds good," I say and let the exhaustion of the day overtake me.

That night, Bren's dad brings over the futon and also Jayce. Apparently, Bren called him to come help. I hate feeling useless, but it is what it is, at this point. Doctors' orders. Before long, I have a small apartment full of people and four pizza boxes on the counter. We all sit around wherever we can—except me, who has instructions to not leave the futon—eat our pizza, and ignore the fact that I am on bedrest until Jayce asks the question I was hoping he wouldn't.

"So, Kat, aren't girls who are pregnant the ones that get put on bedrest? I heard Bren say something about bedrest."

There it is. "Yes, Jayce, girls who are pregnant get put on bedrest when there is a problem."

"So, you *are* pregnant? Do I understand this coded conversation correctly?"

"Yes, Jayce, you understand this just fine. I *am* pregnant, and I *am* on bedrest, and there is a small problem that should go away with the bedrest. Any other questions I can answer?"

I look over to Bren with a stern look, and she shrugs her shoulders and says, "He was bound to find out eventually."

"No, Kat, I think I am out of questions for the moment."

When everyone is done eating, we put together an overnight bag, because without real beds in the place, we decided it would be better to sleep at Bren's parents' house. After arriving at Chris and Tina's house, we settle in on Bren's bed and watch movies the rest of the night.

James

I wake up late on Saturday afternoon and head to the cafe to see how things are going and if Jayce has heard anything from Kat or Bren. When I walk in, Jayce is behind the counter and has a look of shock on his face when he looks up.

"Hey, Jayce."

"Hey, boss man! I wasn't expecting you until tomorrow or Monday. Is everything okay?"

"I sure hope so. How are things around here? Everything been going smoothly with me gone?"

"Yeah, seems like this place runs itself," he says with a chuckle. "I put everything you wanted in the safe, and I didn't have to make much change from it. If you have any questions about how I did it, all you have to do is come ask me."

"Thanks, man, for everything. Hey, have Bren and Kat been in this week? I need to talk to Kat."

"Well, yeah, they have been in here, but I think they spent last night at Bren's house. Kat is on bedrest, and since they don't have much furniture and have a lot of steps to walk up, they decided to stay there until tomorrow."

"Did you say bedrest? Is everything okay?" I ask with a little panic in my voice.

"Looks like Friday her doctor decided she needed it, but I don't know everything. I just found out when I helped Bren's dad move a futon up to their place. You knew she was pregnant?"

"I found out the night of the graduation party. Thanks, Jayce, I am going to head back to the office and see what kind of mess you left me in there."

"Okay, boss, I'll be out here if you need anything."

I go to the office and don't even worry about the safe and what a mess I need to clean up with being gone for a week. My first thought is that Kat needs me, and I need her, and I need to talk to her. I tap out a quick text.

J: Hey you, I am back in town. We need to talk.

K<3: It will have to wait until Monday. I am busy this weekend. Be back around on Sunday late.

J: Not what I wanted to hear. I miss you.

K<3: Miss you too but it has to wait.

J: See you first thing Monday

I don't like it, not one bit.

I need to see that she is okay.

I need to know that she is safe.

I need to touch her.

It seems I have to wait. Frustrated, I decide to distract myself by digging into the books for the week. Luckily, Jayce seems like he has done a good job and has kept everything really neat and organized. It only takes me about three hours to get through them all, and Jayce came in once with a coffee for me and something to eat. I really wish I could hate the guy, for the sole fact he has a thing for Kat, but I just can't.

I help him close up for the night and let him know that he can sleep in tomorrow. I will open up and give him a bit of a break. I thank him again for everything he has done this week and decide that I'm going to give the kid a raise the next time I do payroll.

I walk up the stairs to my apartment and crash. Tomorrow is going to be a long day of making myself busy while I wait for my girl.

Chapter Twenty-Three

Katarina

I wake up on Sunday morning to the smell of an amazing breakfast. When I walk into the kitchen, I am immediately met with a look of frustration from Tina.

"Kat, sweetie, you have to stay off your feet as much as possible. You need to stay in bed. I was bringing breakfast to you," Tina says as I sit at the bar.

"It was fifteen feet. I think it will be okay." A smile crosses my face. It is nice to feel taken care of, to have a mother figure who treats me like a daughter. This is the biggest breakfast I have had since joining Bren and her family. It feels like they're trying to make up for everything I have gone through and the night we are about to have with my mother. I have been trying to ignore the fact that today is the day I have to retell my story—and to my mother, no less.

Bren comes in a few minutes later and we all sit in silence and eat. We settle in for the day watching movies and waiting for my mom's arrival back from her honeymoon. When she finally calls that evening, Bren, her mom, and I load up into the car and make our way to her house. We grab a couple pizzas on the way and get there just as they are unloading the car.

I get out of the car carefully and walk over to my mom to say hi. We all walk into the house and settle in the living room—my choice —and eat pizza while we make idle chitchat.

"Mom, we need to talk; I have a lot I need to talk to you about."

"I know we do. Where do you want to start?"

"I need to start at the beginning. I need to tell you some truths that I have kept from you. I need to tell you how I became pregnant, and I need to tell you it was not my choice. I was raped. Bren and I went to a party one night and I was drinking, and there were drugs, and…I tried to fight, but I just couldn't. I had no strength, and I was so confused, and he just wouldn't listen." I'm rambling it all out and by the end I'm sobbing, and when I look over at my mom, she is crying, and before I know it, she is on her knees in front of me, wrapping her arms around me.

"I am so sorry, Kat. I am so, so sorry I treated you the way I did. Oh, my God, I kicked you out. I am a horrible mother. How could I have done that?" she asks no one in particular.

"Mom, it's okay. You didn't know. You were angry, and I was angry, and no one wanted to listen to the other. Bren and I have done a lot over the last week while you have been away. We have an apartment in the Old Port; it's small, but it will work for us just fine. We'll be okay. Bren and Tina and Chris have been great. I just hope now you understand I didn't want this; this didn't happen because I didn't care about myself or my future. But I want the baby. And I would love to do this with your support and love. I had a job lined up to start tomorrow, actually, but due to some complications, I am no longer able to work."

"Sweetie, what happened?"

"Here is the other part I need to tell you about. After we fought at Bren's party, I ended up at a friend's house, but I felt guilty about accepting his hospitality and was just so low I wanted to be alone. So at one in the morning I decided to leave and was caught in an alley nearby by the guy who raped me. His name is Trent. He threatened me, then hit me in the face so hard I fell down. While I was on the ground, he kicked me in the stomach. I ended up in the ER later that night after James found me outside the alley and brought me back to his place."

My mother covers her mouth with her hand and gasps.

"Does he know you're pregnant?" she asks.

"No, and I would like to keep it that way. Or at least make him believe that it isn't his. Moving on, though—I had a doctor's appointment Friday and was put on bedrest. I have a small tear in my placenta, and they want me to stay on bedrest for at least the next six weeks in hopes that it will heal. So there goes the job I was due to start."

"We will help you, right, Kyle?" She turns and looks at my new stepfather, who has been pacing the floor with a look of murderous rage his face. He hasn't said a word since I opened my mouth to start telling my story. Right then I see the love and concern he has for me. This is the moment I realize I have been awful to him all these months.

"Yes, we will help you. We will help you through *all* this. Have you gone to the police yet?"

Tina pipes in at this point. "No, she hasn't gone to the police. She doesn't want to. There is some justification for that, since he's been threatening her, and if she goes to the police, he'll find out about the pregnancy. I did talk to her about going and talking to someone about her trauma. I was able to get a list of people she can go to. I think if she won't go to the police, she needs someone to talk to, a professional. She's been having nightmares from the whole ordeal."

"I want to move on. I want to make my life worth it, and I want to do right by my baby. I'll go and talk to someone, but mostly I just want to move on and concentrate on what's important. Kyle, I also owe you a huge apology. I have been awful to you, and you don't deserve it one bit. And I'm so sorry, mom; I haven't been fair to you either." I nod over to Kyle. "He isn't as bad as I made him out to be."

Kyle comes over to me, nudging my mom to the side, and gives me a hug. "I really appreciate the apology and understand why you did and said the things you did. Let's start fresh from this point on. I also want you to know I want to kill the guy that did this to you, but on the other hand, I love you like you're my own kid, and I know this has been absolute hell for you. I will be here for whatever you need me to be here for, up and including drowning that guy in his bathtub."

I give a little sniffly laugh through my tears. "Thanks, Kyle. That means a lot to me."

"Now that I have all that out of the way, I do have a question for you and Mom. Do you think there is any furniture that Bren and I can have for our new place since you have to combine two houses anyway?"

"I think we can find some pieces that would work. What do you have so far?"

Bren and I reply in unison, "Air mattress and a futon."

All the adults in the room start laughing at us at the same time. This night is going better than I thought. Mom was so angry at me for being pregnant. Maybe they are right when they say that the truth will set you free.

We stay a bit longer and make plans for Kyle to load up his truck and bring my bed from home and a real couch and another chair of some sorts. I guess I will find out tomorrow what he brings. Bren and her mom decide that she can have one of the guest room beds so that she always has a bed at home. Her dad will bring it over tomorrow around the same time as Kyle, and hopefully between the two of them they can get things up the three flights of stairs, since

I'm useless. I hug my mom tight and tell her I love her and that I have missed her. She tells me to be safe and that she loves me too, and again apologizes for her reaction. After hugs all around again, we go home for the night.

Bren and I make our way to our apartment slowly because she is mother-henning me and get settled for the night—me on the futon and her on the air mattress. One episode of Grey's and I'm out like a light.

I wake up the next morning to a banging on the door, and my nerves go haywire. I guess I'm more afraid of Trent and the man in the suit than I realized. Bren sits up with a start then holds a hand out to me to make sure I don't get up. She hefts herself from the sagging air mattress and stumbles to the door. When she reaches it and opens it a crack, I can't see who it is, but I do hear her say, "Well, well, look who the cat dragged back home."

In that moment, I know who it is, without even hearing his voice. All the anxiety in my chest turns to butterflies. Bren opens up the door after releasing the chain, and in walks James, looking sexy as hell for being so damn early in the day. He is bearing coffee in each hand. He hands one to Bren and then walks straight to me on the futon with that smoldering look on his face and bright, ice-blue eyes. He offers me the other one with a look so tender I almost cry.

"Hi," is all he says as he looks down to me, and I can feel my cheeks start to hurt from the huge smile on my face. I don't know how long we stayed like that, looking at each other, but apparently long enough for Bren to put on some clothes and brush her teeth, because she is walking out the door, calling over her shoulder, "I'll be at The Java if you need me."

I am left all alone with James, and I'm not sad about it.

James

Sunday comes and goes, and I keep myself busy. When I close up Sunday night, I make my way to my apartment once again, and this time, I can't sleep. This time, I prepare for the morning, when I get to go see Kat. She doesn't know this, but I know where she lives, and I know she will be home.

I decide that I will be bringing the first present I had planned on giving to her on her birthday and saving the Tiffany's bracelet for another time, once I get a feel for her and if she wants me beyond friendship. I plan on opening up the cafe on Monday, and once the morning workers show up and are settled for the day, I will go to Kat's apartment with a coffee and her necklace and grovel for her to accept me. I want to tell her everything—apologize for taking off, especially when it seems like she needed me most.

I will win her love, and I won't stop until I do.

I can't stand it anymore. I have to see her. I make a couple of coffees, the girls' usual order, and ask Jayce the apartment number, then walk out the door. Since I know the owner, and I live in the building right down the street, he's entrusted me with a key to the building in case there is an emergency and he can't get there. I'm calling this an emergency. I let myself in then jog up the three flights of stairs and down the hallway to their door and knock.

"Well, well, look what the cat dragged back to town," Bren says to me as I hand her the coffee I brought for her and walk straight over to where Kat is and hand over hers. Time seems to have stood still as I look at her into her eyes, hoping that she can see what I feel for her. Before we know it, Bren has just closed the front door and left, saying she will be at my cafe if needed. I swear, this girl turns me back into a teenage boy who doesn't know how to talk to girls.

"I brought you this," nodding to the coffee in her hand, "and I also brought the birthday present I never got the chance to give to you that night." I hand her the wrapped package as I take a seat next to her and watch as she opens it. She carefully unwraps the box, and when she pulls off the lid, her eyes go wide and she covers her mouth and gasps.

"Oh, my God, you didn't have to get me something so nice."

"Oh, Kat. I want to give you the world. I really don't think you know how I feel about you. You consume my thoughts. It killed me being away from you this past week, and it killed me even more knowing that you needed me and I wasn't here. I want to protect you, to take care of you. Hell, I want to be your knight in shining armor. "

I am looking at her in her eyes as I speak and notice a lone tear fall from her eye and wipe it away.

She has her arms wrapped around my neck as she says, "Those words are so sweet, James. I wish I could allow you to be my knight, but I can't. I have too many demons following me to put all that on you. I care about you so much, and I don't want you to look at me differently, but I need to tell you how I came to be pregnant." My heart sinks to my stomach with her words, but I let her continue. "James, Trent is the father, and not by choice. One night Bren and I were at a party, and I got really messed up. I was drinking a lot, and smoking pot, and then someone offered me cocaine. I didn't realize how trashed I really was, and when Trent started flirting with me, the attention felt nice. But pretty quick things got too intense, and he wouldn't stop, I didn't have the strength to push him off and no one could hear me crying because the music was so loud. He raped me, James. He took my virginity that night, and he left me pregnant. "

"I'm going to kill that bastard." I stand up and start pacing her small space. I would kill my father all over again in this moment, if I could. This is my fault, and I need to do something. I need to tell Kat the truth, even if she will hate me for it. I stop pacing and look at her with tears streaming down her face. "Kat, this is in no way your fault, but I will make him pay."

"James don't do anything stupid. I don't want to do anything about it, because the last thing I want is for him to know that I'm pregnant. I want to move on from this. But I also can't be with you the way you want me to be. James, I'm pregnant, and on top of that, I have been told to stay away from you or else something bad would happen. I don't know who it was, but I had a note handed to me here at my place by a guy in a black suit. He said nothing, handed me the note, and walked away. There was a check for $25,000 in there. I'm scared, James. That kick in the stomach caused some damage, and I'm on bedrest for the next six weeks. I need everything to stop and calm down so I can take care of me and the baby. I need to keep all of us safe, and that means you need to stay away, for the sake of all three of us. I'm sorry, but that's the way it needs to be. I'm so sorry."

I pull her into my arms and kiss her forehead, wanting to cry myself at how she's been hurt because of me. I kiss each eyelid as I wipe the tears away from her face, and then I kiss her like I have wanted to do for so long. I pull back and look her in the eyes. "Kat, most of this situation is my fault. I left this past week to try to protect you and this world I want with you. I found out so much, and I'm doing everything I can to do put to right. I will make Trent pay for what he did. Trent will never know that this baby is the result of that night, and I won't be going anywhere. I will keep my distance from you in the eye of the world, but I will be here for you always."

"James, please I love you for this, but I just need you to go, please," she begs me, tears streaming down her face. She tries to walk away into the bathroom, but I stop her. I take hold of her face and kiss her with everything I have in me.

I pull back, still holding her face in my hands and say, "Kat, I love you. I don't know when it happened, but it did. I will go because you asked me to, but know this, I will make him pay, and I will love you always. I will be waiting for you to let me back in when you're ready." I kiss her again, and when I pull back, I let go of her beautiful face and walk out the door. It about breaks me to close the door and hear her sobbing on the other side. I stand there listening to her cry for I don't know how long before I finally leave.

When I get back to The Java, I see Bren at the end of the counter, talking with Jayce, their heads close together. *So maybe I was wrong about him, because it looks like he is very into Bren.* I walk over to Bren and grab her attention.

"Kat needs you, but please know this, I love her, and when she is ready for me in her life, I will be waiting for her." Bren has a shocked look on her face, and I walk back to the office to make a phone call to my newfound brother.

Chapter Twenty-Four

Katarina

James closes the door, and I break—I sob, and I am angry with myself for letting him walk away. He loves me, and I basically told him that I love him, but I can't put him in danger. I won't cash the check, but I will stay away from him to keep him safe. Not too long after James walked out the door as I requested, Bren is back, bursting through the door, panting.

"What the hell happened in here? James is Hulking out, but also looks like someone ran over his puppy. You don't look much better than he does."

"I may not cash that check, but I will keep him safe, and to do that I need to keep him away from me. I told him about Trent and the note left to me. He told me everything was his fault. I don't get it, Bren. What am I missing? How can Trent be his fault?"

Bren comes over and wraps her arms around me. "I don't know, sweetie, but we need to take care of you and your baby, first and foremost. You know, he told me he loved you, and that he will be waiting for whenever you are ready."

"I know he does, and I love him too. I don't know when it happened, but I do, I love him. It killed me to tell him to go, to tell him that I couldn't be with him. But, Bren, what if the threats are true? What if someone wants him that badly that they go through me? Bren, that makes me scared for both of our lives, and yours too."

"Somehow, I think he will get it all figured out, Kat. He doesn't seem the type to leave it be. He wants you; he loves you. He knows what happened to you, right?" I nod my head yes. "He still wants you after knowing what happened. Kat, I don't think you should make him wait for too long. He was made for you, and I believe you were made for him."

"Bren, I think you may be right, but I'm still scared. I need to worry about me and the baby before I worry about a guy. Let me get through bedrest and make sure everything is okay, and then I will see, okay?"

"You better hope that James has patience, because that is still another five weeks or so. I have a feeling that he will be on my heels as much as he can to find out about you. But I will do what you say. Five weeks of bedrest and then see what happens after that. If you are okay, I am going to head out for a bit. Need me to bring you back anything?"

"Thanks, but no, Bren, I am fine. I think I am going to go and lay down for a bit before everyone is here with furniture for us. Thanks, though."

Bren leaves and locks the door behind her, and I walk over to the window and look over Old Port. When I look to the street, I notice someone looking up—Trent. I quickly jerk away from the window. *What the hell does he want now?* I take note of his appearance on the street and then go to lie down for a bit.

About two hours later, I am woken again by knocking on the door. At this point in my life, I never know who it's going to be. I place the chain on the door quietly and slowly open the door the width the chain will allow. Once again there again is a guy in a black suit looking at me. I go to slam the door shut when a hand pushes against it.

"Miss Kat, don't be alarmed. I was sent here by Mr. James. He had a feeling I would scare you, so I wanted to introduce myself to you. But if you want me to stand out here while you message Mr. James, I don't mind waiting."

"I will be right back," I say and close the door. I send James a text.

K<3: man in suit at my door. You send him?

About thirty seconds go by before I get a reply.

J<3: Yes. I will protect you even if I can't do it myself. Max is your bodyguard. I love you.
K<3: How do you even have access to a bodyguard?
J<3: I will explain it to you when you are ready to take a chance on me. Until then please trust me. I need you safe.
K<3: Okay, thank you.

I go back to the door and open it all the way and let in Max. He is tall, full of muscles, and sporting short hair. He is actually really hot, and I hope Bren can behave herself. He sure looks like a bodyguard.

"Come in, Max, I am sorry. I wasn't aware that you would be coming, but it looks like we are about to spend a lot of time together. I am on bedrest and can't really go anywhere, so I apologize for the boring job you have encountered here."

"Miss Kat, there is no job that is boring if I am protecting and keeping my boss's loved ones safe."

Max almost reminds me of a gigantic teddy bear; he's huge and walks with a swagger, yet has this feeling about him like he has a heart of gold. I think just by initial introductions I am going to like him. But I also don't want to waste his time when I just need to stay in one place for a while and stay out of anyone's eyesight. "Max, first of all, please stop with the Miss Kat thing. Exactly what do you plan on doing while you are working? I mean, I have to sit around and do basically nothing for the next five weeks. Will you just sit around with me, or out in the hall, or I don't know...I've never had a bodyguard before, I don't know how it all works. "

"Okay, Kat it is, then. I can be in here, or I can be in the hall by the door. I don't mind, as long as you're safe and I can do my job."

This is going to take some getting used to—and I can't wait to see Bren's reaction. Speaking of Bren, I hear her at the door. She stops in her tracks as she sees Max standing there. "Um, Kat. Did you know there's a huge hottie in the house?"

"James sent him. Meet Max, my new friend—or bodyguard, as I was told."

"Why on earth did he get you a bodyguard? What kind of trouble are you in?"

"Well, I told him to leave me alone, that I needed space from him, and in return, his idea of protecting me is to send Max over to babysit—" Max coughs and stares. "Sorry, Max. I mean, guard me."

"Okay, so what is he not telling us? There has to be a reason that he would send Max here, other than to just be his replacement protector. I'm going to go talk to him." She turns around quickly before I can stop her and walks out the door with a Mama Bear look in her eye.

James

When I get back to my office, I pick up my phone and dial my brother. He answers on the third ring.

"Hey, James, you get your girl yet?"

"We have a problem. That note and guy in the black suit scared her to the point she won't have anything to do with me. She won't let me near her, and she is on bedrest because of an injury from the night Trent attacked her. I have more information about that, too. My bastard of a father got her *raped* by that asshole. She is pregnant because Trent raped her at a party one night. I don't know if it was his initial intention or order per se, but it still happened. For all I know he was hired to get close to her to distract me away from moving forward with anything with her and took it way too far. I want to kill Trent; he doesn't deserve to live."

"Whoa, wait, let me get this straight. Trent raped Kat while on our father's mission to keep her away from you?"

"That's what it seems like."

"Is he still bothering her? Does he know he is the dad? *Fuck.*"

"Kat won't let me near her. I need to make sure she is safe. Do you have anyone we can put with her until we can get this shit straightened out?"

"I still have Max in the area. He's like a brother to me, we've known each other since we were kids. He already knows her, and I actually checked today to see if she has cashed the check just to make sure, and she hasn't. I honestly think she is trying to protect you by staying away. I will get a hold of Max and send him over to her place, but this time we need her to know he is there. He is a big guy, but he is one of the few that have a heart. He will make sure that she is taken care of while you aren't allowed to. Now, don't be surprised if the girls have a reaction to Max—I hear he's a favorite with the ladies. But I'd be more worried about her friend Bren," he says with a chuckle.

"Thanks, man. I know we don't know each other well, but I hope we get the chance to change that. Now, what do we do about Trent? I want to make sure he won't bother her ever again, even if I have to do it myself this one time. For her, I will do anything."

"I will get my guys on it and make sure he knows who he is dealing with this time. Just keep an eye out, man. Let me know if you see him around. We will destroy him and make sure he never knows that baby is his."

I hang up the phone and go about my day the best I can. I walk out of my office to the counter and go through the motions of pulling an espresso. When I turn toward the front window, I see red. Well, actually, I see Trent, across the street, and he is looking up. It dawns on me why he is looking up—he is looking at Kat's apartment. I go back to my office and call my brother back.

"He is watching her apartment from the street *right now*."

"Max is on his way up now. Stay away from him, we will get that bastard. No worries, Brother."

I get a text message from Kat as I hang up the call. Max is there, and she is confirming I sent him. Thank God she has a brain in her head. I shoot back a reply, ending it with *I love you.*

I thought that when my father died, I was done with all of this shit, but it seems to be getting worse. About thirty minutes later, Bren walks into my office like she owns the place, and she doesn't look happy.

"Why does Kat need a bodyguard? What aren't you telling her?"

"Bren, she won't let me look after her right now, and I need to. Can you leave it at that?"

"Fuck no! Tell me what is going on and tell me now, before I call the cops. Is it about that fat check in her purse?"

"Bren, please, don't call the cops. I will tell you, but please don't tell Kat. She didn't give me a chance to talk to her about all this before she asked me to leave today."

"Talk."

For the next fifteen minutes, I fill Bren in on my entire life story, ending it with my father's death and my half-brother's succession to the throne. She stares at me for a moment, likely wondering if I am telling the truth or if I have completely lost my mind. Eventually, after opening and closing her mouth like a fish out of water, she speaks.

"Wow, okay. I get it. You need to tell her eventually, but I get why you want to wait. I will just tell her that you sent Max because you can't watch out for her. She thinks something else is up, though. But, James, she is like a sister to me, and I want her safe too, so please let me know if I can do anything. Please keep me in the loop."

"Bren, I appreciate who you are to Kat and how much you care. Like I said before, I love her, and I will swear to you, she will be safe. You both will be. I swear to get that bastard, and I swear to you that she will be happy in the end. I hope with me, but as long as she is happy, I will be happy."

"Okay then."

Bren leaves after our conversation, but not before she grabs a free coffee from Jayce, and I am back to it, trying to let Jackson handle it all and not lose my mind. It is only just after lunchtime, and it's going to be an even longer day now, with everything going on. Mid-afternoon, both Jayce and I take off for the day. He tells me he's heading over to help move furniture into the girls' apartment. Thank God for that; Kat needed something comfortable to sleep on. I was about to go buy a bed for her this afternoon. I go to my apartment and do some laundry and little things around the house, since I've been gone for a while. Nothing helps. Nothing makes this day any better. Nothing makes me forget the look on Kat's face when I left this morning. So now, I wait for the phone call to give me an update.

. . .

It seemed like days before I hear anything, but in all reality, it was just hours. Apparently, Trent has gone rogue; he is no longer on the mission that was ended the day my dad died. Jackson told me he was going to send a couple of his guys up to help out and to get to Trent. He wants answers as much as I do. I am really beginning to like this new brother of mine.

Chapter Twenty-Five

Katarina

A couple of weeks have gone by. Mom has been by often, bringing Max and I food or a little something for me, like a soft lap blanket or fuzzy socks. When she first came over and I had a beast of a guy hanging out, she immediately questioned who he was and why he was there. I really didn't have much to tell her, but Max, being the great guy he is, was able to put her at ease. I've had a lot of conversations with Mom, and I've told her all about James. She was a little concerned about the note I received and the fact that Trent is still hanging around. Max was again able to reassure her that with him there nothing will happen to me.

My relationship with mom has changed, and we are finally able to have the relationship I've been wanting again. I need my mom by my side. Bren is great, but there is nothing like your mother when you're pregnant and navigating through life as a mom to be.

We have our furniture, and I finally have a comfy place to sleep and relax during the day, and a small table where we can sit and eat. But with the furniture came a lot less space to move around, and

Max is a big guy. I have come to call him Teddy Bear since he is so deceiving with his looks and how he actually is. He is such a kind, sweet guy. We have been playing a lot of cards, watching a lot of movies, and even talking about ourselves. I've told him about what has been going on with me, and I have also told him that I have noticed Trent outside on the street a few times since his arrival. This is when he reassures me that no one will harm me or my baby. Speaking of the baby, I have actually been on bedrest for a month now, and we get to go to the doctor today to see if the tear is any better.

"Max, are you ready to head to the doctor?"

"Yes, let me go grab the car and bring it around. Lock the door with the chain behind me, and I will be right back."

Max leaves, and I do as he says, locking the door and latching the chain in place. Five minutes go by, and I hear a knock on the door. It seems too soon to be Max, but I open it up anyway with the chain still on. I just learned a good lesson: don't assume it is who you are expecting, because it probably isn't. Trent is on the other side of the door and slams into it with his shoulder, snapping the chain and knocking me down to the floor.

"I knew he had to leave your side eventually," he snarls at me, and with one arm he hauls me up off the floor, throws me over his shoulder, and walks out of my apartment. I'm kicking and screaming, but that doesn't last long, because he drops me on the floor and wraps a bandanna around my eyes and in my mouth, gagging me. Once again, I am over his shoulder, and we are going out another door at the other end of the hallway, leading to a different exit than Max would use.

Trent drops me in the back seat of his car, and I start kicking out at him and try to escape out the other door. This time when he drags me close, he punches me in the face, effectively knocking me out. I come to a few minutes later, my arms now bound together and still blindfolded. I stay quiet in the back seat as he drives us about another ten minutes. When he stops, he yanks me from the vehicle, again throws me over his shoulder, and goes down a set of stairs of a nasty-smelling house. I get thrown down on an ancient couch. He ties my feet together with a rope I feel scratching at the skin on my ankles, and it hurts. He removes the bandanna covering my eyes, and as I suspected, this place is filthy and dark—likely a basement. I don't bother to make any sound, and I try and stay as calm as I can.

"You are mine now, bitch. I've wanted you since that night at the party. You didn't think I would forget, did you? We're going to make a call and get your lover man all worked up. For what he did to my family, he deserves everything he gets."

I have no idea what he is talking about, but I continue to stay as calm as I can. He grabs his phone and starts to dial a number. When the person on the other end answers, he puts it on speaker so I can hear.

"Hey, James, this is Trent. I have something you may want."

"Where is she, what did you do to her?"

I hear the panic in his voice, and tears start to form in my eyes. I haven't spoken to him or seen him in five weeks, and now all I want to do is hug him and never let him go. *Why was I so stupid to push him away?*

"She's just fine. I just wanted to let you know she is mine now. You can go to hell."

"Let me talk to her. I need to know she's okay."

"Sure thing, but you will never find her. She will be gone before you can even find this place."

"What do you mean, gone? What are you going to do to her?"

"I guess you will never know. But the three of us will be fine without you."

Alarm shoots through me as I realize he knows about the baby. He removes the gag from my mouth and holds the phone close by. I take a long breath, steadying myself before I speak.

"James, I'm okay. I'm not hurt."

With panic in his voice and rage he tells me, "Kat, I'll find you. I love you. I will find you."

"I love you, James." Right then, Trent disconnects the phone, and James is gone.

Trent puts the gag back in my mouth and starts to pack things up. I sit there watching him and try to figure out how he knows about the third person in the picture when someone else walks into the basement. *Jayce.* My eyes go wide, and I try and gasp, but I can't with the damn gag.

He looks right at me and says, "I see you have finally made it. Did the guard dog let down his guard?"

I have never seen the look in Jayce's eyes like I do right now. I want to know what is going on, but I have no voice. At this point, I can't control my fear anymore. I'm terrified, and feel so betrayed. Jayce walks over to me and removes the gag as soon as I agree not to scream.

"What are you doing, Jayce? Why?"

"Oh, Kat—sweet, innocent Kat. What you don't know is that my dad was one of James's biological dad's lackeys in Boston. He was second-in-command. Your boy destroyed him when he brought his brother in to take over the family. As a result, the week after James got back, my dad was found dead by apparent suicide. They all but pulled the trigger for my dad, and I want revenge. I knew that Trent was working for Mr. Milano, so when he was relieved of his duty, I took over and started to pay Trent to get to you. But then James put that guard dog on you, and we never had the chance until today. Bren told me you had an appointment, and it worked out perfectly. Now I get to take you and his baby away from him while James suffers."

They don't know it's Trent's baby. I feel a rush of relief. I have to keep it that way, no matter what. They think that they are taking away James's baby. I play along with it. It looks like my only chance to save us. I play it off like I know what he is talking about when he talks about the Milano Family. I honestly have no clue. Nothing he just said made any sense to me.

"What are you going to do now?" I ask.

"It is time to go to Boston and see about making a trade with Jackson. It is time to see how much your life is worth," Jayce answers.

Who is Jackson? Then it all clicks as I play back what Jayce said. Family, Boston, Jackson—this is the mob they are talking about, a mob family. *Why is James mixed up in a mob family?*

I am picked up off the couch and pushed in the direction of the door back outside. This time, we get into another car, and I am shoved in, making me lie down across the back seat. No one can see me from this angle as we drive.

Nothing is said the entire ride to Boston, until we arrive at our destination. I know they were ready and waiting for us at the Milano house by the reaction heard from the front seat. I'm still flat in the back seat. I almost expected them to speed in the opposite direction, but then I hear the sound I dread—the sound of two guns being cocked and ready to fire. "Climb over the seat and get between us," Trent barks. I follow orders, and as soon as I have my butt in the seat, Trent flings open the door and drags me in front of him as a shield. Before I know it, I have Jayce next to me, and we are walking to the door like it is a normal visit to a friend's house. We are let into the house and led to an office. I gasp when I see it's occupant, who looks so much like James it could be his twin. Is it his twin? I'm so confused.

"Jayce, I assume, and Trent hiding behind Miss Woodbridge, would be my guess," the guy says with a sexy, deep voice.

"Who are you?" I ask, since the gag was gone.

The sexy guy walks around the front of his desk and stands right in front of me with a kindness in his eyes. "Miss Woodbridge, I am James's half-brother, Jackson. I have heard a lot about you. How are you doing? Do you need any water?"

I notice as he speaks to me, his eyes keep looking down, like he is trying to tell me something.

"You're looking a little faint, my dear."

Then it clicks. With an air of exaggeration, I sink down to the floor and try to brace myself as best as I can without being obvious that I'm not really out.

In an instant, the room is surrounded by what seems like a hundred feet from my vantage on the floor. I am quickly scooped up and moved to the other side of Jackson's desk, and when I look up, I see Max. He must have been right on our tail to be able to get here so fast. "I'm so sorry, Kat." He looks at me like he is hurting and disappointed in himself. He unties the ropes on my wrists and stays in position, making sure I don't get hurt.

"Max, it isn't your fault. I checked to see who was on the other side of the door before opening it, and he kicked it in." A gunshot rings out through the room, and Max covers my body with his. A few moments later a guy yells, "All clear!" and Max peers over the desk then helps me to my feet. Trent has a few bruises on his face, blood dripping from his mouth, and is down on his knees, holding his stomach. Jayce, on the other hand, has a gunshot wound in his shoulder, and is also down on his knees, his jaw clenched in pain.

"Trent, James is here to finish what we started. He wanted to have a turn with you, and I'd hate to deny him the satisfaction. Jayce, you will be dealt with as well. You think that shoulder is painful? It's just the beginning," Jackson says with steel in his voice.

Things are becoming clearer for me. I don't know if it is for me or if it is for himself, but now I have a better idea of what has been going on and why Max became a permanent fixture in my life. I am sitting at Jackson's desk when James walks in. He takes my breath away even though he looks like shit... but in a sexy way. I haven't seen James in almost a month, and I blame that on myself. James looks tired and worn out; he even looks like he has lost some

The Night He Saved Me

weight. I knew I'd done that to him by causing all the worry. He looks at me, and a ghost of a smile passes his lips.

"Jackson can we take this outside? Kat has been through and seen enough today, and she doesn't need to witness anything else."

"I agree. Boys, take the trash to another location."

A chorus of "Yes Boss," can be heard as they remove them from the office and James starts to follow. Jackson goes to the side bar and gets a bottle of water for me. As he hands it to me, I grab his attention.

"Jackson, they both think I have James's baby; neither have any idea about Trent. Please let James know this." He nods his head and makes his way over to James, pulling him aside to whisper in his ear before he leaves the room. With a nod of his head, James leaves. Sitting here with Jackson, no words are spoken, but the silence is heavy. I don't know what James is doing in the other room, and honestly I don't care as long as those two men never bother me or my baby again. A short while later James returns, looking Jackson directly in the eye with a murderous glare, giving him a message before he softens his look when he turns in my direction.

"Jackson, they are both all yours to do with as you please. Just make sure we no longer have to see or worry about them again." James walks over to me and takes my hand, pulling me into his chest and wrapping his arms around me. He then lays a sweet kiss on my forehead before turning to Jackson. "May we borrow a room for the night? We will head back to Portland tomorrow after breakfast."

"Sure thing, brother," Jackson replies. "Dinner can be brought to your room, if you need it, or you can join me in the dining room, just let me know in a little bit. Kat, it was nice to finally meet you."

"Same to you, Jackson. Thank you," I reply, and then we walk upstairs to one of the many bedrooms in this beautiful house on Beacon Street.

189

James

When the door closes behind us and we are alone for the night, I finally speak to Kat. I feel the rage leave my body as I look at her, her eyes so kind and the gentle swell of her belly making her look even more beautiful than ever. I wrap my hands on either side of her face and place a light kiss to her lips.

"Kat, my God, I was so scared today. I am so sorry my life has done this to you. Everything is my fault. I wanted to explain it all to you the night you told me about Trent, but you wanted me gone. Kat, I am so sorry for this."

"James, I'm fine. They didn't hurt me. Scared me, pushed me around a little, but no one ever hurt me."

"Kat, you don't understand. You being pregnant is my fault. You being threatened is my fault. Everything is my fault because of who my father was. Trent was on my father's payroll. His job was to keep you away from me. Because of me, Trent went after you and did what he did. Kat, you were *raped* because of me, because my father wanted me under his thumb. I left to go find Jackson, the brother I never knew I had just so I could get away from all of this. I can never express how sorry I am but, Kat, I am here, and I will always be here for you. When Max called me today, I was in the car so fast. I needed to get to you. I love you, Kat, and I will never let anything happen to you again if you will let me."

"You are not to blame, James. You are not your father, and I have seen what you have done to stay away from this life. You left to find Jackson so you wouldn't be trapped here in the position he is in now. I don't know if you did it for me or for yourself, but I trust you, James. I don't blame you for anything. Your dad, Trent, and Jayce, are all sick people. They did this, not you. James, I love you."

"I love you too, Kat."

I take her face in my hands and kiss her slowly, lovingly. Kat wraps her arms around my waist, and with her touch, I deepen the kiss, putting every emotion I feel into it. We are sitting on the edge of the bed, and I slowly push her down, wrapping myself around her. I have no intention of making love to her, since I know she is not cleared by her doctor; I only want to hold her. Kat makes it so difficult to not go further, but I have to resist.

"Kat, I want more than anything to make love to you, to show you what sex is supposed to be like, but we can't. You need to be cleared by the doctor. I know you had an appointment today. Right now, I just want to feel you in my arms and take care of you."

"James."

Before she can say anything else, her stomach growls loudly.

"I think I need to feed you," I say with a chuckle. "I'll call Jackson and have some dinner sent up."

"Thank you, I haven't eaten all day. But, James, I want you to know I love you, and I appreciate you thinking of me first. I want you. I want to feel loved by you."

I kiss her quickly on the lips and smile, this time with a glint of mischief. "I'm gonna love you so hard you'll forget your own name."

Chapter Twenty-Six

Katarina

One of Jackson's people brings us up an amazing dinner and we sit and eat in bed. After eating, we set the plates to the side and curl up together. I want to love this man with everything I have, but I can't —not yet. We lie in bed, wrapped around each other, talking about anything and everything, and I fall even deeper in love with him. For once in my life, I feel loved unconditionally for who I am. I love the feel of this man in my arms, and I don't ever want to let him go. We are both tired and can feel sleep taking us over when his phone starts to ring.

"Oh shit!" he exclaims. "I'm in so much trouble."

"Hello, Bren!" he answers, and then winces when her voice blares through the phone.

"Is she okay? What happened? You never called!"

"Bren, Kat is fine, we're here together right now. I'm sorry I didn't call earlier. Things were kind of nuts. We will be back tomorrow."

"You suck. Let me talk to her."

James hands me the phone, and I say, "Hey, Bren."

"Are you really okay? I have been terrified all day. I can't believe he didn't call me back!"

"Bren, I am fine, I am here with James and feel safer than I have in a long time. We need to talk when we get back, though. But don't worry, I'll see you tomorrow. James needs to talk to you before we hang up. Love you, Bren."

"Love you too, Kat."

I hand the phone back to James. "Bren, once again, I am sorry, but I had to take care of Kat. Is everything going okay at the shop?"

"Yeah, everything is getting cleaned up now, and I will lock up. What about the morning?"

"That is what I wanted to ask you. Are you up to opening the door in the morning? You won't have to do anything; Grace will be in and can do everything. You just need to let her know the drawer is the same from today."

"I can do that for you. Just keep Kat safe and bring her home."

"That I can do. We should be back before noon."

"Okay, see you tomorrow. Night."

"Thanks, Bren, night."

James sets the phone down on the nightstand and turns off the light. He leans over to me and kisses me lightly on the forehead.

"Let's get some sleep, Kat. It has been a long day."

"Sounds good."

I lean over and kiss him, and in my next breath, his tongue is sliding across my bottom lip, trying to get me to open for him. I allow it, and we kiss slowly for a few minutes before I feel the rush of passion surge through my body. This kiss has more emotion in it than I have ever felt in my life. We start to slow the kiss down and pull away from each other. The lights are out, but I can still feel his eyes on me. James pecks me on the lips once more and then pulls me into his chest, giving me another kiss on the forehead as we settle in for the night to sleep.

I wake the next morning to silence—no sign of James anywhere. Once I am done stretching like I have never stretched before, I get up and make my way to the bathroom that is attached to the bedroom. At some point last night, James was able to find me a shirt to sleep in. Once I get done in the bathroom, I curl back into bed. Not more than a minute later, James comes walking in with a tray of breakfast. He sits on the edge of the bed next to me and sets the tray off to the other side and leans in to kiss me.

"Good morning, sweet girl."

"Well, good morning to you too, handsome."

"I brought you breakfast, want some?"

"Smells great, what do you have?"

"I brought a little bit of everything. Eggs, bacon, toast, fruit, and some French toast. I hope there is something that you will like here."

"Good news is I like everything you brought, but I think I'll go for the French toast and some fruit." I peck him on the lips, and he sets the tray on my lap.

While I am eating, he lets me know the plan for the day. We are going to go back to Portland after we get cleaned up and dressed. I finish eating, get dressed, and am ready to go. We walk downstairs and meet up with Jackson.

"Thank you, Jackson, for everything. I hope we have the chance to get to know each other better soon," I say.

"I hope so too, Kat. I am glad that you're okay. I am so sorry that you have been dragged into this mess." He gives me a hug and whispers in my ear, "Now get this guy looking human again and give him a chance." He pulls back and winks at me, then says to James, "Take care of her. If you need anything, let me know. The trash has been taken care of and shouldn't be a problem for you any longer." He grabs James's hand then pulls him in for a bro hug, complete with back pounding. I shake my head a little. Men.

"Thanks, Jackson, good to know. We will see you again soon—I hope on better terms next time. Thanks for everything you did yesterday."

"No problem, brother. Have a safe trip home. Max has insisted on driving you both home, and he is ready and waiting in the car."

We all say good-bye again and walk out the door. Once we are settled into the back seat together, I ask James for his phone. I missed my appointment yesterday, and I need to reschedule as soon as possible. Once I locate the number and make the call, I have a new appointment set for four this afternoon. When we get home, James carries me up to my apartment so that I can take a shower and put on some clean clothes. After I'm all ready, we go over to his place so he can do the same. Once we are both back to being human, James takes me to the coffee shop so he can check in. Bren is there at the counter getting a crash course in the art of making coffee from Grace.

"Oh my God, you are back, finally!" Bren exclaims as we walk in the door. Bren comes rushing over to give me a hug, then looks me over to be sure I'm unharmed. Once she's confirmed I am okay, she looks to James. "Thank you for bringing her back, and here are your keys. I need a nap."

Bren gives me another hug and then grabs her bag and heads out the door for her nap. Once James checks in with Grace, he leads me to his office. "I have to catch up on a few things, and then I will take you to your appointment. Do you mind hanging out for a while? I really don't want to let you out of my sight right now."

"That's fine, James. I have to stay off my feet anyway, until I am cleared from the doctor, so I'll just make myself at home in this big comfy chair."

James gets his work done and then we go to my appointment a couple hours later.

I'm nervous as we settle in the waiting room. "James, I wouldn't be surprised if they ask if you are the dad. I haven't been to this office before."

"Kat, it is okay. I honestly wish I was the father. No matter what, I will be there for both of you for as long as you'll let me. I will let you decide what I am to your child, though, so I will follow your lead today."

With those words, he just melted my heart. I wish he were the father too. Today, I won't even cross that subject unless I need to. I just need to make sure that the little one is okay. But I do let James know what he just did to my heart.

"James, you have no idea what your words mean to me. I so wish things were different, but your words make me fall even deeper for you. I love you, James."

When my name is called, I feel the hesitation from James if he should stay in the waiting room or come with me, so I take his hand and lead him back with me. I go through the normal routine, cringing a little at the scale. Once we are in the room, the nurse takes my vitals and measures my stomach before assuring me the doctor will be in shortly. Sure enough, the doctor comes into the room moments later with the ultrasound tech behind her, pushing the ultrasound machine.

"Hi, Kat, I'm Dr. Johnson. How are you doing today?"

"I really am feeling good. I'm ready to get off bedrest and back to normal as long as I can before the baby comes."

"Well, everything else is looking good. Let's get you lying back so I can take a look."

Dr. Johnson feels my stomach, lets me know that my uterus feels like we are measuring correctly, and then she brings the tech over to take a look inside. She puts the cold gel on my stomach and starts the machine, running the wand across my stomach. Before too long, I hear the heartbeat, and it is a strong one. I take a look over at James, and the look of wonder on his face as he stares at the monitor melts my heart. A few minutes go by and the tech finishes her measurements. She brings Dr. Johnson over and points at a few images she had taken.

"Kat, from what I see here, it looks like the tear has healed on its own. That is great news. On to other matters. It is usually a bit soon, but would you like to know the sex of your baby? We seem to have gotten a clear shot today."

I look over to James, and he has a huge smile on his face, and I know in that moment he is the father that matters in this baby's life. He catches my eye and he nods. He really reminds me of a giddy schoolgirl with his expression on his face.

"Yes, Dr. Johnson, we want to know."

I catch the surprised look on James's face when he realizes I have said *we*, not *I*, but I continue to go with the flow of the appointment.

"Well, Kat, you are measuring eighteen weeks and four days now, and from the picture we have captured here today, you are going to have a little girl. Congratulations."

The tears are instant, the moment she says what I will be having. I look over to James, and he has tears in his eyes too. *I'm going to have a little girl.*

"A girl. We're going to have a girl."

"Yes, Kat, you will be having a girl," Dr. Johnson says with a slight chuckle to her tone. "Kat, I want you to know that the tear is healed, and I will take you off bedrest, but I still don't want you to lift anything or do too much. Before you even ask, yes you may have sexual relations but try not to be…what's the word I'm looking for? I guess aggressive." She laughs.

"Thank you, Dr. Johnson. I am so excited, and I will be careful in all areas suggested."

We head out of the office after checking out, and when we get to James's car, he turns me around and kisses me so hard and fast he takes my breath away. When he pulls away, he just looks at me with a smirk on his face. "A girl, who will be as beautiful as her mother," he says.

He helps me get into the car, and we head toward home. When

he pulls behind the alley to park, we get out, and again, he takes me in his arms and kisses me, this time not fast and hard, but still with all of his emotions pouring out into this kiss. When he pulls away, he settles his hands on my cheeks and looks right into my eyes.

"Kat, I need to close up the shop tonight, and I need to get some work done before that. I want you to go and celebrate with Bren, and tomorrow you're mine. I wish I didn't have to work, but I do. Will you be okay, or would you like me to walk you up to your place?"

"I'll be fine, James. Go do your work, and I'll go find Bren. I will see you tomorrow, just let me know what time."

James pulls me into his arms and hugs me. When he pulls away, he kisses me on the forehead—his signature kiss for me. Reluctantly, we head in separate directions.

James

We are back to reality, minus a few people who needed to be gone.

Once I get the drawer figured out from the day before when I had to take off, I am free to make my calls. I have a plan, and I need help.

I dial Jackson, and he answers immediately, "J, is everything okay?"

"Everything is fine, I just need a favor or two. I am planning on asking Kat to move in with me tomorrow, and I plan on taking her to the park where I found her after her birthday party. I'm planning to bring a picnic lunch and everything, just a nice date day, but I need help in my place. I want to change my guest room into a nursery, but not decorate it now—just get the crib, changing table, and the comfiest chair possible. I won't have any time to do all that between now and before the date, because I want to bring her back and have the place all set with candles and a romantic dinner catered and the bedroom for the baby set up. I don't trust anyone else to help me. Do you have any guys in town still that could help get the place set up and let the caterers in?"

"Max is still in town; I think he has a thing for your girl's friend Bren. Why don't I call Max and then have him get a hold of Bren, and then they can work together to get it all set up? Who do you want to bring the food? And any idea what furniture you want? You just worry about the date during the day, and we will get the rest taken care of."

"Thanks, Jackson, I like your idea. I was thinking the Old Port Bistro for food. I also got a Tiffany bracelet when I was in New York for her. I want to marry this girl, and I will one day, but right now I want her to have a place that is safe for both her and the baby, with enough room. I will send you a link to the furniture I want so you can pass it along. I'm sure Bren will have fun with this. I just feel bad about taking Bren's roommate away from her, but I think she will understand. Well, I hope so."

"You got it, James, I'll have Max call Bren to get it all set up. You just worry about your date; come back to your place around six tomorrow."

"Sounds great. Thanks, man." I get off the phone with Jackson and go out into the cafe. I am greeted by Bren and Kat, who are standing at the counter.

"Hey, ladies. I thought I sent you to celebrate?"

"We *are* celebrating. I needed my one coffee allowed each day, and then we are finally going to go shopping and maybe even buy a baby girl outfit."

Bren pipes in at this point. "I'm so excited I'm going to have a little niece. Time to spoil her." She is bouncing on the balls of her feet, clapping her hands together with as much as excitement as anyone else. This time of day I have another girl working, and Bren questions it, "Hey, by the way, where is Jayce? I haven't seen him in a few days."

Kat and I both look at each other and decide in just one look that

200

we need to tell Bren what happened. I suggest we head back to my office to talk and hopefully not ruin the day for her and Kat.

"Bren, we have to tell you about what happened and who took Kat the other day. It wasn't just Trent; Jayce was involved. Actually he was the mastermind behind it. You know I told you about my family, while I was trying to keep Kat safe? Apparently my dad had hired Jayce's dad as his right-hand man, and when things went down, and my dad died and Jackson became his successor, Jayce's dad lost it and killed himself. Jayce blamed me, and even though Trent wasn't on the payroll anymore to hurt Kat, Jayce put him on her. Trent grabbed Kat, and Jayce brought them to Boston. Now, the only thing I can say is that Jayce and Trent won't be a problem for anyone ever again."

Bren sat for a moment, clearly stunned. "Oh my God. I can't believe it. *Wow*," was Bren's response.

"I know you liked him, Bren. I'm sorry it ended up being this way." Kat leans over and gives her best friend a hug.

"That explains a lot, though. I thought Jayce was still into Kat, with the amount of questions he would ask me about her. I guess it makes sense now. I just wish I knew how to pick a guy who isn't after my best friend to hurt her. Too bad; he was kinda cute."

We all laugh at that. Bren took the information a lot better than I thought she would. I send the girls out to enjoy the celebration of Kat having a little girl and go about the rest of my day doing what I can in the shop since we were now short an employee. I close up for the night, do the drawer, and then lock up and head up to my apartment. Once settled in, I text Kat about tomorrow.

J<3: Be ready by 11
K<3: Okay! Luv U. Night!
J<3: Love you too. Night.

I get ready for bed and introduce my head to a pillow.

Chapter Twenty-Seven

Katarina

After leaving The Java, Bren and I headed to Target to get some of the things we have been talking about to decorate the apartment. When we got there, she received a text she wouldn't tell me about, but I saw a sly smile on her face. I figured if she wanted me to know she would tell me.

After Target, we moved on to the outlets in Freeport and did some baby shopping. I am so beyond excited to be having a little girl. I have had so many different emotions over this pregnancy, but now I think that I am completely ready to take on the challenge.

Bren was like a mad woman, running around and looking at all the baby clothes, picking things up, saying how tiny and cute they all are.

I walk over to a display of newborn clothes and pick up this amazingly soft pink jumper. I know that this is what I need to get her. There is also a matching headband, and I decide I'll splurge and buy both. When I look over at Bren, she has her arms full and looks at me with a *what* expression on her face when I stare.

"I told you I was going to spoil her."

"That you did, my friend," I reply with a laugh.

We both check out at the register, and I honestly have no idea what all she bought. Once we are back in her car, it is most definitely dinner time, and we decide to go grab some food at the local chowder house in Freeport. Once we are seated and get comfortable, we can finally talk about everything that has been going on.

"Bren, you sure you are okay about Jayce? I had a feeling that you guys might start to date. I know you liked him more than a friend."

"Kat, you're right; I honestly thought that we might be heading somewhere, but obviously I was wrong—he was using me to get to you and James. I will be okay. He was just a guy. I am more concerned with you. Are you sure you are all right? I see the sad look in your eyes sometimes."

"Bren, I am sad sometimes, but I will be okay. It just sucks that I finally find a guy like James, who has been by my side through thick and thin, and he isn't even the dad. I see it in his eyes, too—he wants to be the dad. When we were at the doctor's office, and they asked me if I wanted to know the sex, I said yes *we* would. It scares me how much I see him as the dad, but he hasn't run away with any of what I told him, and he is still here by my side, as if he really was the father. Sometimes I worry if it's the guilt because of his part in everything. Bren, what do I do? I don't know what happened to Trent, nor do I want to, but when this baby is born, what do I do? I can't list Trent as the father, but I can't list James, either, can I?"

"Kat, I would just leave off the father's information on the birth certificate. You and James aren't married, and what happens if you two split up? Just be the only parent on the certificate. It will make things a lot easier, and then if you get married down the road, you can have James adopt our baby girl."

"Kat, this is why you are my best friend. You seriously always know what to say to me. I know we've had our share of bad moments over the past few months, but in the end, you have always been there for me."

Once we were finished, we headed back toward Portland and our little apartment. I get a text from James telling me what time to be ready tomorrow, and Bren also got a series of text messages that she refused to explain. I ended up saying goodnight to James while Bren continued texting away with a goofy grin on her face.

The next morning, I wake up and stretch. I pick up my phone and notice I have a text message.

J<3: Good Morning. See you at 11

I shoot back a quick reply.

K<3: I'll be ready.

Then I notice the time and let out a little scream. My alarm didn't work, today of all days! I have an hour to get ready; I can't believe I slept that long. Once I'm out of the shower, I grab my favorite jeans, but they won't fit. Since I have been on bedrest, I have been wearing yoga pants that stretch, and now I realize I have nothing I can wear except maybe a dress. I hope my dress fits until I can go and get some new maternity clothes. I find the least form-fitting dress in my closet—a flowing maxi dress—and it fits. Thank God for that. I've never been too into the whole makeup and hair thing, so I call for Bren to help me.

"Bren, you out there? I need your help."

A perky Bren comes bounding into my room, fully dressed for the day and suspiciously giddy. I'm really starting to wonder what is going on with her, between the mysterious text messages and today's behavior.

"What do you need my help with, Kat?"

"James is picking me up in about thirty minutes, and I need to do something with my hair and makeup. Can you help?"

"Sure, what are you two up to today?" She glances down at what I'm wearing. "Oh my God, where did that belly come from?"

"First, I have no idea what we are doing, and second, I know; I have no real clothes that fit me anymore. I need to go shopping for new stuff ASAP."

Bren works her magic, doing light makeup and flat ironing my hair. The lob cut I got for my birthday is starting to grow out, and honestly, on a good day, it looks a mess. Thankfully, Bren knows what she is doing and gives me a beach hair look with just enough curl and mess. As soon as we walk out into the main room, we hear a knock at the door. That boy sure is punctual. I grab my bag, slide into my favorite pair of flats, and answer the door.

"Beautiful," is all he says, with that look on his face like he wants me as bad as I want him.

"Why, thank you. I am starting to feel like a whale."

"Shut up, Kat, you do not look like a whale!" Bren yells from the couch, ever the supportive friend.

"I agree with Bren, you are most definitely not whale-like." He leans in and kisses me on the forehead like he always does. "Are you ready for our day?"

"I sure am. Bye, Bren, see you when I see you."

"I don't want to see you until tomorrow," Bren yells back over to us with a wink.

James takes my hand in his and leads me out of my apartment and to his car. I have no idea where we are going, so I'm just along for the ride. As I sit there holding James's hand, I start thinking about all the things I'm going to need for both myself and the baby.

With all the drama, I haven't had much time to really think about that until now. Apparently, James notices my mood change and squeezes my hand. "Everything okay, Kat? You look sad all of a sudden."

"I'm fine, James, just thinking. I've had a lot going on, my sleep hasn't been the best because I've been having nightmares, and I'm going to need a lot of things soon for this little one. Not to mention I have no clothes I can wear anymore. You may start seeing this dress every day for a while," I joke, but he grows serious.

"You will have everything you need for her and you. I will make sure of it. Please don't worry about that. I've got you, forever and always."

I tear up, which happens a lot these days. "You're too good for me, James."

"I just want what's best for you. What can I do to help the nightmares go away?"

"Just having you around helps, James. But I have been talking to a counselor; she was coming to the apartment while I was on bedrest. It seems to help more and more each time I talk to her about what happened at the party and in the alley."

"I'm glad you have someone to talk to and it's helping, but please know I'm here, and you can talk to me anytime."

"I know, James, and maybe I will one day, but I'm not ready to talk about it with you right now. I'd much rather enjoy our time together and leave that part behind us. My counselor is helping, and having you in my life helps too."

"Okay, just know I'm here."

We continue our drive in a comfortable silence while I sit here and question what I did to deserve this guy after everything that has happened over the past few months. I honestly don't deserve him, but I sure am lucky to have him. I squeeze his hand back and decide to enjoy the day, because I can't change anything right now. When I look up, we are pulling into the park where he saved me that night, the night I wasn't completely right in the head. The night that changed my life with James. Today will be a good day. And I decide I am going to enjoy whatever he has planned.

James

I don't like the look Kat has on her face, like the world is weighing on her shoulders. I try and reassure her that I'm here, and she has nothing to worry about, and it seems to have worked. I can tell that today she has realized she can't wear her clothes, and I plan on changing some things around today to fix that for her. We pull up to the park, and I see her eyes glow with recognition. I run to her side of the car and help her out. Her belly has seemed to grow overnight, but I'm smart enough not to comment on that. Once Kat is on her feet, I kiss her forehead and tell her to wait right there for just a second. I run to the back and pull out the picnic basket and a blanket. The weather is gorgeous today, with just enough breeze to keep the heat comfortable. Once I make my way back to Kat, I grab her hand and lead the way to the bench where we sat that night. This place is special to us, and I want her to remember this day.

I lay the blanket on the ground and help Kat sit then take my own place across from her and open up the basket. I have packed us sandwiches and chips, sparkling apple juice, and fruit salad. Nothing fancy, but all put together by me.

"This is amazing, James, thank you."

"There is no need to thank me. I would do anything for you."

We sit and eat and drink from champagne flutes I packed. When we're finished eating, I pull Kat into me, and we sit and look out over the water. It seems like forever since it has just been Kat and me, with no interference from anyone or anything. We sit like this for what seems like hours, talking about anything and everything.

We even start talking about names for the baby. When the topic changes to the baby, I try and act as excited as she is, but deep down I'm sad. The baby isn't mine, and she won't be when she arrives on paper, but I already feel like she is mine. The reality of it is what makes me sad. Kat can tell there is a shift in my mood and sits up to look at me in the eyes.

"What is it, James? I thought you were excited about the baby?"

I grab her face and peck her lips before speaking, "Kat, I am excited about the baby, but I am also sad about the baby, for selfish reasons. She isn't mine, and I want her to be. I have to remind myself I'm not her father, and when I do, I get sad. Does that make any sense?"

Kat places her hands on top of mine and kisses my lips softly. "James, as far as I am concerned, she is yours and always will be yours. You prove to me all the time how much you care about not just me but her too. Biologically she isn't yours, and that makes me sad too. But we can't change that. I don't plan on listing a father on her birth certificate; there is no reason to. But with no dad listed, James, you will be able to adopt her as your own if the time comes. I want that. I want to be a family with you. Please know that." Kat kisses me again, and this time I deepen the kiss. Kat knew exactly what to say to bring me out of my head. I know we are at a public park in the middle of the day, but I lay her down gently and kiss the hell out of her. I behave and keep my hands PG, but my brain has gone X-rated on me, and fast. I slowly pull back to calm myself and pull Kat back into a sitting position. I kiss her forehead and get up and gather our things.

"As much as I loved our time here, and I plan to continue that kiss later, behind closed doors, we need to get moving to the next thing I have planned."

We get everything loaded back into the car, and I help Kat in. While I am walking around the car, I shoot a quick text to Bren.

JMAN: Where do I take Kat for new clothes?
BGirl: Motherhood Maternity outlet in Freeport
JMAN: Thx

I get in the car and grab Kat's hand as we pull away. "Ready to shop?" I ask her.

"Shop? What are you talking about?"

"I want to take you to get some clothes you can wear that fit. I told you not to worry, that I will take care of you."

"No, I can't let you spend money on me like this. The necklace you bought me has been plenty for me, not to mention this wonderful day." She fingers her necklace as she says this.

"Please let me buy you a few things; it will make me feel better."

"Fine, just one outfit. I will buy more later with my money."

I agree to her terms, but I also don't let her know that it isn't going to happen that way. She will have everything that she needs and even a few things she wants. Once I get to the place Bren told me about, we walk in hand in hand.

"What do you need the most?"

"Since I couldn't put my jeans on today, I'll have to say jeans, and a shirt to cover my belly, unless everyone wants to see it hanging out in a few weeks."

We are approached by an employee, asking if we need any help. I reply, "Yes, please, my Kat here needs a new wardrobe for the remainder of her pregnancy." If looks could kill, I would have been dead in 2.2 seconds.

Under her breath and with that glare, she hisses, "One outfit. I told you one." I ignore her and follow the sales girl around the store, dragging Kat behind me. After about an hour, Kat has been fully matched with a maternity wardrobe, in spite of her fervent protests. We walk out of the store with four bags of clothes. I set the bags in the trunk of my car and then help Kat back in. I get a text from Bren as I go around the back of the car to my side.

BGirl: all set! caterer is on their way up. ETA?
JMAN: Just leaving Freeport see you in 30 or so

I get into the car and look over to Kat. "I hope you aren't too mad. I wanted you to have what you needed. I love you."

Her look softens a little. "I know you do, James. I love you too. What I don't like is not being able to do this for myself. How will I be able to take care of a baby if I can't even buy my own clothes?"

"Kat, please don't worry about that. You have what you need today because I wanted to, not because I felt I needed to. I bought you these clothes because I love you. I don't expect anything in return."

"I'm sorry, James. I let things get the best of me sometimes. I love you." She leans over to give me a quick kiss. We are then on the road back to my place and for the grand finale of the day.

After parking behind the building and helping Kat out of the car, I lead her to the door of my apartment, arms full of bags. It has been so long since she has been here. I missed her being in my space. When I reach the door, there is a note addressed to Kat.

I love you! Kat have fun and don't come home ;)
Bren

"Looks like I have been ordered to stay at your place."

"Seems that way. What a good friend you have there," I reply with a smirk. But what Kat doesn't understand is that, in a way, this is a letter of permission for her to say yes.

I open the door and am met with candles lining the edges of the stairs. I open the door wider so Kat can see and usher her in the door while her mouth hangs open wide.

"Oh my God. Who did this? It is beautiful." Looking at me, she asks, "Did you plan this?"

"Kat, I have been planning this the last twenty-four hours, with a few people's help. Now, let us go inside to see what else there is."

Leading Kat up the stairs and into my apartment, I notice that in the dining area there are roses all over the place, with one lying across what I assume is to be her plate. The music is low and beautifully romantic, and as I seat her, a waiter comes walking in, dressed nicely but not in a tux. They followed my instructions for this not to be too fancy and to focus on the romance of it.

"Good evening, sir, ma'am, I am Brian, your server tonight. Can I start you off with a drink? Sparkling apple juice, water?"

"Water is fine for me. How about you, Kat?"

"Water please."

Brian goes to get drinks, and Kat looks at me with a question in her eye. "James, what do you have planned for tonight? Because whatever it is, you hooked me the second we walked in here. This is beautiful, so romantic. Thank you."

"This is just the beginning, Kat. Just wait for dessert." I wink at her. She gets my innuendo and blushes, saved from responding by Brian returning with drinks and some warm bread. "Dinner will be out in a few minutes; can I get you anything?"

"No, thank you, we are fine right now," I answer back. Brian leaves, and I take Kat's hand from across the table. We continue with the meal, and it is delicious. Seafood chowder and corn chowder were brought out. We both tried a little of both and talked and ate bread. Once we had moved onto dessert, I realized that my time had come. I walk over to the side bar where I knew Jackson had set the bracelet and the key with a ribbon attached to it and kneel down by Kat's feet.

"This is not a proposal—before I completely freak you out," I say with a wink. "I want you to know how important you have become to me and my life. I was so lonely before I met you, and before I knew what was happening, you had consumed my every thought.

We have gone through so much the past few months, and I wanted to show you how much I appreciate you." I pull out the wrapped box with the Tiffany bracelet in it and set in her hand. "Open it."

Slowly, Kat opens the package, and I already know she is shocked because she recognized the Tiffany Blue box. "You didn't have to buy me anything more. You know that, right? But I won't refuse something from Tiffany's." She winks at me. She opens the lid to the box and gasps softly when she sees the rose gold bracelet with the diamond. Tears start to shine in her eyes, and she blinks them away. She looks at me and then lunges at me, wrapping her arms around my neck. "Thank you, James. It is gorgeous. I love it. It is perfect."

I kiss her softly and then pry her off me and set her back in her seat. "I have one more thing for you. More of a question, actually. I wanted to know if you wanted to move in with me. I know you just got a place with Bren, and I know it may seem too soon, but I want you here in my space. I want to love you and protect you, and I want you by my side every night and every morning. I want to take care of you, and I want to take care of your little girl. I love you Kat, and I love your baby. Kat, will you move in with me?" I present her with the key for my apartment with the bow attached.

Tears are flowing, and her body is wrapped around mine on the floor. She pulls my face to hers and kisses me, then I think I hear a yes before she kisses me again. I pull away slightly, laughing, and ask, "Was that a yes?"

"Yes, yes, yes! We will move in with you, James." And then she kisses me hard and fast. I have to pull back from the kiss when Brian comes back in and clears his throat. "Sir, are you by chance ready for dessert?"

I help Kat up off the floor and get her seated before I answer, "Yes, I think we can go for some dessert." Brian quickly retreats back to my kitchen and returns with two plates of cheesecake. One thing Kat and I agree on is cheesecake is the best kind of dessert. With a perma-smile on her face, she eats her cheesecake. Shortly before we are done, Brian and another guy slip out of the apartment like stealthy ninjas in the night. We are all alone now, and I can finally have my girl.

Chapter Twenty-Eight

Katarina

This day has been wonderful. I couldn't have asked for a better guy to come into my life. James had the most perfect night planned out, and he also asked me to move in. Once I read the note from Bren and walked into the apartment, I knew something was up and she was a part of it. I was too excited and happy to put a second thought into moving in with James. I knew Bren would be happy for me. Heck, I think she knew something would happen between James and me because she had it set up for me to not have to pay for anything in the apartment. She also knew she would be close to me. Bren was smarter than anyone gives her credit for.

As James and I sat there eating our dessert, I notice the two guys leave, and this is where I start to get nervous. Don't get me wrong—I want James so incredibly bad, but I worry about actually doing it. I hardly remember the first time I ever had sex, so I am nervous. Once we are finished with dessert, James gets up and takes my hands, pulling me up out of the chair and into his chest.

"We're alone now, finally." He lightly kisses my lips, running his tongue across the seam of my lip trying to get me to open, and I do. I want this with James, but as much I have the urge to jump him, I also am scared. The kiss intensifies, and he leans down grabbing behind my knees to pull me up around his waist. I lock my ankles together, and he starts to walk toward his bed. Once we reach his destination, he turns around and sits on the edge of the bed and pulls away from the kiss, setting me on my feet so I'm standing in between his legs.

"Kat, I want you so badly. I have dreamed about this. But I also want to move on your terms, at the pace that you set for us. If anything is happening you don't like or want to do, please tell me."

"I will. Now I want to feel you. Lift your arms."

I take off his shirt and admire what I see. Then he does the same to me, running his hands up my legs and slowly pulling my dress up and above my head, discarding it to the side. I am standing there in my bra and panties, pregnant belly hanging out, making me a bit self-conscious. But not after he leans down and kisses my belly, mumbling the word, "Beautiful."

James stands, taking possession of my lips as he gently moves us onto the bed with his body covering mine. He leans down, keeping his weight off my body, and kisses down my neck then over my collarbone and to the tops of my breasts. He glances up at me, asking for permission with his eyes. I nod my head and he starts to push my straps down, slowly exposing my breasts. When the lace material is gone and my bra discarded to the side somewhere, he rolls his tongue around my right nipple while palming the left. My back arches because it feels so good. I have never been touched like this by any guy, and I am glad that I have James to share this moment with, this experience with.

James continues his exploration, looking up and making eye contact with me every time he does something different. James is now kissing right above the waistband of my panties. He lowers his head between my thighs and brushes his nose over my panties, over my center. A flash of heat pulses within me at his touch. He then kisses me again above my panty waistband before looping his thumbs into the sides and tugging them down, scattering kisses as he goes.

I am now completely bare to him. James spreads my legs apart and licks me. His tongue meets my clit slowly, circling around until he has me squirming. He then inserts a finger slowly, pumping in and out. After a few strokes he adds a second finger. Soon my body is tightening up, and I feel the tingle all the way into my toes. I arch my body into him and yell. "James! *Oh God,* James!"

He continues what he is doing until all the waves of my orgasm, the first I have ever had, subside to a low tremble. He leaves me breathless. I open my mouth to speak. "I have never felt anything like that before in my life."

James is now eye level to me, giving me one of his many looks, and this one I can't figure out. "You have never had an orgasm before, not even given by your own fingers?"

"No, that was my first," I reply, shyly hating to even admit it.

"I hope it to be the first of many to come," he says as he slides his jeans over his hips, sending them to the floor. He stands at the foot of his bed, wearing just his boxer briefs, and asks a question. "Kat, before I go further with you—I am clean; I was tested last month and haven't been with anyone since the moment I saw you. But I will use a condom if you want me to. What do you want me to do?"

"I want you to come here, and I want you to make love to me. I've been tested too, I'm clean. I want to feel every part of you."

James quickly removes his boxer briefs and slides up my body, his skin creating a delicious friction that sparks heat all over again. When we are eye to eye, he asks me, "You okay?"

"Please, James, no more questions. I'm fine. I want you inside me now."

James kisses me and inserts his fingers inside me again,

caressing me. Once he decides I am ready, he pulls back and slowly pushes himself inside. He is so large I am unsure if he will even fit, but he does, and once he is all the way in, he stays still, waiting for me to adjust.

Slowly he starts to move, and I'm in awe of how beautiful this is and how much I want him. I start to move my hips along with him and encourage him to go a little faster. He does. The feeling I had earlier starts to return, and I am panting now, working toward it like a finish line. He feels so good. He leans down to my ear and says, "Baby, I am so close. You feel amazing wrapped around my cock. Are you close?"

With those words from him, I tighten my grip with my legs and urge him on. "God, yes. So close, James, so close. Don't stop."

He speeds up a little bit which throws me over the edge, and then I'm hurtling to an even stronger orgasm than the first. My mind is whirling that it can even be better than it was, but it is. He continues to pump inside me then groans, "Oh, God, Kat, I'm coming." Once we both still, he leans down, breaths still coming fast, and kisses me softly.

We lie there for a long while still attached, savoring the aftershocks from the most amazing orgasm. James has given me such a gift, a knowledge of how good sex can be with love between two people, and it's healing my mind in ways I didn't expect.

He gets up out of bed and goes into the bathroom. I hear the water running, and a few minutes later he returns with a warm wet cloth and cleans me up. Once I am clean, he gets back in bed, covers us up, and pulls me against his chest. He kisses me on the forehead and says, "I love you so much, Kat. That was amazing. Now sleep."

"I love you too, James. 'Night." I burrow into him and get comfortable. I couldn't have asked for a better day or night. I will never forget it.

James

Last night couldn't have gone better. I woke before Kat this morning and put together breakfast in bed for her—nothing fancy, just fruit and a muffin from the coffee shop. When I arrive back to my room, she is just starting to wake up. Kat has the biggest smile on her face, and I nearly burst with pride at the knowledge that it was me who put it there.

"Good morning, love."

"Morning. Is that for me?"

"Of course it is." I walk over to her and place the tray next to her and kiss her softly on the forehead. She takes the tray, puts it on her lap, and digs in. While Kat eats, I go take a shower and get dressed. When I return, she is making her way to the bathroom in a hurry. She lifts up on her tiptoes and pecks me on the lips before she dips under my arm to enter the bathroom and closes the door. "I'll be right out."

When Kat emerges from the bathroom, she grabs a bag of her new clothes and gets dressed, murmuring happily about how comfortable her new jeans with a stretchy waistband are. She's so cute I can't stop the grin on my face. But, I have another surprise for her, and I can't wait to show her. I grab her hand and start to guide her out of my bedroom, soon to be ours.

"I have a surprise for you, Kat. Come with me."

"What have you done now, James?"

"You'll see in just a second."

I lead her to the door of one of my two guest rooms. "Close your eyes." She does, and I open the door. I guide her in. "Open your eyes." She is in front of me, so I don't see her face, but I hear her reaction.

I hear a gasp and then she says, "Oh, my God."

Kat turns to me, tears streaming down her face. I hope they are happy tears. Surely I didn't screw this up. "James, I can't believe you did this. When?"

" After we found out the sex of the baby. Once I made calls about getting everything set up for last night, I made the arrangements to get this for you. I knew I was going to ask you to move in, and I wanted you to know I wanted *both* of you here with me."

She leans up on her toes again and says, "Thank you, I love it all." She follows with a kiss so soft and full of love.

"I want you to decorate this room however you want, but I wanted to have the furniture you need for her."

"James, it is all so perfect. I love the white finish and the modern design. You did amazing with your choices. Thank you."

We head down to the cafe so I can check in with my workers and then make our way to her apartment to tell Bren the news about her moving out. As expected, she is fine with it and tells Kat that she made the right choice. The girls gush about the nursery room and furniture and start to plan how to decorate it. Kat decides that Bren can keep all the furniture and the bed that is already set up in her room, so all Kat has to pack are clothes and bathroom things. Within half an hour, we have everything packed up and ready to go. When they were packing, I made a call to Max and asked if he could come over and help us. He quickly agreed and arrived right as the girls finished packing. I notice Max and Bren exchanging heated looks and wonder if Jackson was right about Max's interest in her. Max is a good guy with a good heart. Bren could definitely do worse.

The four of us carry everything—well, mostly Bren, Max, and I, since Kat isn't supposed to lift anything—and put it all into my room. While the girls start to unpack, Kat notices that I have already made room for her things and that her maternity clothes have already made their way into the closet. "Confident much, James?"

"Hey, when I know what I want, I go after it." I wink at her, then Max and I leave the girls to it and go grab some coffee in the kitchen. "So, Bren?" I ask him, eyebrows raised.

"Nothing to tell. She is a nice girl, though."

"You'd be good for her."

"I sure am going to try. That girl is a tough one to get through to, though."

I agree with him then drop the subject. I thank him for everything he has done for Kat and me over the past weeks, and ease into conversation about the Boston Red Sox. The girls are back out in no time, and we all head down to The Java. This has been the most perfect twenty-four hours, and I hope it keeps getting better. I may not have been looking for a girl, or even a family, but I am sure glad I now have a reason to live my life and not to just exist in it. Kat and the baby have saved me from a lonely life. My heart is now full of love.

Epilogue

Katarina

James and I have settled into a good pattern over the past few months living together. My mom and Kyle love him, as do Bren's parents. After the events that took place at the beginning of the summer, I am so glad to finally feel normal again. Bren and I have been decorating the nursery, and it's so beautiful, with soft pink and purple everywhere. Bren threw me a small baby shower where I was able to get the big things I needed, like a car seat and stroller from both Bren's parents and my own. Jackson showed up about a week ago with a bundle of baby goodies, including a Pack 'n Play and more toys than she could ever need. Both Bren and Jackson are so excited to be getting a niece and are spoiling her rotten before she even gets here. I'm about a week away from my due date at this point, and everyone is on full baby alert. I can't even text a hello to anyone without getting a "Is it time?" in return.

James has gone to every appointment with me, and every time he sees her or hears her heartbeat, he gets teary-eyed. I love seeing him this way; it just shows me how much he loves me and my baby girl.

It doesn't matter how she came to be a part of my life; he has embraced both of us far more than I could ever expect him to.

We are now into the colder months. Thanksgiving has passed, with all our families joining together, plus Max, since he has decided to stay in the Portland area. I honestly think Jackson is paying him to keep an eye on James and me to make sure no one bothers us again, but it is nice to have him around. He has become a part of our family. I also think he has a thing for Bren. The way I catch him looking at her sometimes reminds me of the way James looks at me. Bren seems like she likes him, when she lets herself. Something is going on with her, and I wish I knew what it was. She has been pulling away from me, but if she needs me, she will ask. I am always here for her, just like she has always been there for me.

My bag is packed and in James's car, along with the car seat, ready for Baby Girl's arrival. No one knows her name, and it is driving everyone crazy. James and I know, obviously, but everyone else will find out when she arrives. They know we are having a girl, and that's enough for now. I'm sitting around watching TV, when I decide I need to get up and move. I feel like a house, with feet I can't even see anymore, but everyone says I am looking good, and James is always saying how sexy I am. If only I believed him. I walk down to the cafe to see James; I would rather check in with him in person than text him. He has made this new rule that I need to send him a message every two hours unless we are together. He is crazy, but I love him and so I'm humoring him.

I get to The Java and find him behind the counter, so I waddle my way over to him and wrap my arms around his waist, giving him a kiss. "Checking in, boss." James laughs and kisses me on the forehead.

"Thanks, babe. I'd much rather see your face than a text. How are you feeling today?"

"I feel fine, but I am so ready for her to be here."

"Me too, my love, me too. Why don't you go sit down, and I will bring you your coffee allotment for the day?"

"Thanks, babe. I love you." I make my way out from behind the counter and over to my 'spot'—a comfy chair I had him add to the seating area. I am about to sit when I feel a rush of liquid between my legs.

"James, can I get a rush on that coffee and a ride to the hospital too?" I yell over to him. He freezes, and when he notices the mess on the floor he goes into overdrive. Thankfully, his other worker has the right mind to finish my coffee as James runs to his office for his keys and wallet. She brings it over to me and drops a handful of paper towels on the floor before heading to the back for a mop. I look at her and wince. "Sorry!"

"Kat, it's fine. Not like you meant to break your water on the floor. Good luck! I can't wait to hear the news of her arrival and a name."

"Thanks, Cindy. I will have him call in when we have news." Then I see the tornado coming my way, snatching me up like I weigh nothing and carrying me to the car. He sets me in gently after I remind him to grab the towel I have purposely set in the back seat. Off we go to the hospital. We are in the car about two minutes when I get my first hard contraction. James looks over at me with near-panic on his face as I wheeze and pant to get through it. A few minutes later I get another one; they are four minutes apart, by the time on my phone. Pulling up at the curb of the hospital, he gets me out, along with my bag, and rushes me through the door, leaving the car running in the circle drive. I really hope he doesn't think they have valet parking here. We finally get to the maternity ward, and he starts to calm down and goes back to park the car. I think knowing we were where we needed to be helped calm him.

The nurse gets me all settled into a room and hooked up to the monitors. Next on her list is to insert the IV into my arm. Thankfully, I was able to drink my coffee on the way here, because now I am limited to ice chips. Once I am settled and James has moved the car to a parking spot, we start to make the calls to everyone. Actually, it is more like one mass text message.

James: We just arrived at the hospital. Kat's water broke.

Many replies start to flood his phone, all the same message from each person, saying, "On the way."

Shortly after the mass message, my doctor arrives and decides to check my dilation. I am moving along fast and am already at 8 centimeters, so our baby girl will be here sooner rather than later. By the time family starts to arrive, they are told to stay in the waiting area, because the doctor now has me pushing. In a matter of ten minutes since I was first checked and a lot of hard painful contractions, I have reached 10cm. I only had to push for another ten minutes—though they were the hardest ten minutes of work I've ever done—to have my beautiful baby girl in my arms and tears in my eyes. James is right next to me, eyes filled with tears as well. He leans down and places a kiss on her forehead, like he has done with me from the start. "You are beautiful, and I love you," he whispers to her.

The nurse comes over to us and asks to take her to get her cleaned up, and reluctantly, we let her go the few feet away from us. When she is returned to my arms, she has a tiny little pink hat on and is wrapped up in a blanket. I get cleaned up a little bit while James holds her, and then we allow the family in to meet our beautiful little girl.

Once the door is opened, the room fills with people: Tina and Chris, my mom and Kyle, Jackson, Max, and Bren. I announce her name to our wonderful friends and family. "I want you all to meet Stephanie Elizabeth Russo." I decided to automatically giver her James's last name because I hope he will be the only father figure she will ever know and love.

A chorus of acceptance comes from the crowd. James reluctantly allows each person to hold her, and when she is returned back to my arms, I breathe in her sweet baby smell and sigh. Slowly, after a while, each pair starts to leave the room and head home for the night, allowing us to get some rest. Jackson hangs behind, and I notice he hands James something. I don't question it but focus on my beautiful Stephanie as she sleeps. Jackson says his good-bye and is the last one to leave. James walks over to me sits on the edge of the bed and again kisses my forehead.

"Kat, you did amazing today. I love you so much." He pecks me on the lips and continues. "I want you to know how much I love you and Stephanie. You two are my world now, and I will forever be here to love and protect you both." He strokes a finger across her cheek and looks up at me again. "I want us to be a family in every way possible. Kat, will you give me your heart for the rest of your life? I've already given you mine. Will you marry me?" He pulls out the blue box Jackson had just given him and opens it to show a spectacular diamond Tiffany ring, exactly like I had described to Bren. I wish these darn tears would go away, but they won't, so with blurry eyes, I look at the love of my life, the man who saved me from myself, and say the only thing I can say.

"*Yes.*"

∽♡♡

Turn the page for a sneak peek of book 2, *Fighting to Save Me.*

Sneak Peek

FIGHTING TO SAVE US, A SAVED BY LOVE SERIES BOOK

Prologue

There was a time when I was happy; my friend Kat was responsible for that. Kat made me look at life differently. We shared an apartment after we graduated from high school. That was until James came into her life and they moved in together and had a little girl. I was thrilled for her but also a little sad for myself. A family of my own was something I wanted, although it felt like perhaps would never happen.

Then Max walked into my life. He is the definition of sexy, with his tall and lean frame, short hair, and steely gray eyes that look like a storm brewing, but he has a heart of gold. He is also the one of the most feared bodyguards for the Milano family, but if he cares for you, he is just a giant teddy bear. I have come to call this trusted and loyal man a friend. He was assigned as Kat's bodyguard for a time, and I grew to like him—maybe more than like. We hooked up a few times after Kat moved out. I was relieved to know that he would be staying in Maine and not returning to Boston with Jackson, his boss. Things seemed to be going great with everyone. Finally, I was happy.

Until that one day I went to the doctor and my life changed forever.

❦

Six Months Ago

It's a perfect winter day in Maine. The holidays are here, and the entire family has gathered to celebrate Christmas at my parents' house. Kat and James came along with his brother, Jackson, from Boston. Max also came to my parents' house, because since he became Kat's bodyguard last summer, he has become family. Kat's mom and stepfather joined us also.

We weren't always this close—a lot has happened in the last year. I think we have all come out better on the other end of things, a closer and a bigger family. The vibe is full-on holiday spirit, with the Christmas tree lit up, a fire going in the fireplace, and Christmas music streaming through the speakers.

The girls are in the kitchen baking cookies and chattering about the upcoming birth of Kat's baby girl.

"So, Kat, when will we get her name?" my mom asks.

"Not until she is here. That's when we will announce her name to everyone."

"That isn't fair; we want to know. I'm her grandma, I should get to know," Kat's mom whines.

"I'm sorry, but it's our secret to tell when she arrives," Kat says, a devious look on her face.

"Where are those cookies?" James hollers from the doorway. "We are hungry men out here."

Kat goes over to him, wraps her arms around his waist— the best she can with her belly in the way—looks up at him, and replies, "In a few minutes. We are almost done decorating them."

He kisses her forehead like he always does and holds her for a minute before retreating back to the guys. I stand there looking at them and dream about a day where I will have someone who will love me that fiercely. I've had no luck with any boy that has crossed my path. The last two guys I had an interest in were horror stories: one raped my best friend and the other pretended to be friends with us so he could sell us out to the mob. Not a great track record.

Our night goes by too fast; the cookies are all gone except what's left for Santa, which we've left on the fireplace with a glass of milk. My mom insists that we still hold this one tradition in this house. I think it's cute and humor her every year. My parents' house is large, so we all stay the night so we can wake up Christmas morning and open presents together. I love this big family we now have, and soon we will have one more to add. I have a feeling we will all be focused on her next year.

The next morning, we all open presents and ooh and ahh over each other's gifts. I sit back and watch for a few minutes, relishing the love that is in this room, though it makes me a little sad. I want a family of my own one day, but recent developments have made me all too aware that a family might not be in my future.

Once dinner has been served, as well as dessert, everyone starts gathering up their goodies to head home for the night. I stand at the door and say my goodbyes to each pair that leaves through the front door. Max and Jackson are the final two. I hug them both, but when Max hugs me, his hold is a little tighter than the rest.

He whispers into my ear, "Merry Christmas, Bren." When he pulls back, he sets a small box in my hand with a smirk and turns to leave.

I stand there in shock as I watch them retreat to their car. I look down at my hand and hesitantly open the lid, gasping at the sight of a round diamond attached to a delicate chain. I look up to try and catch them, but they have already pulled out of my parents' driveway. *Why would he give me such a beautiful, expensive gift like this?* Slowly, still in shock at his gift, I close the front door and make my way back to the kitchen to help my mom clean up.

Chapter One

Bren

It has been six months since Christmas and the day Max gave me my diamond necklace. I wear it every day. Six months that I have kept my secret, gone to many doctor's appointments, and lived a quiet life, separated as much as I can from the ones I love.

Max has asked me out on dates here and there, but I've turned him down every time. I've thrown myself into my studies and even made sure to take an extra class this semester to make me seem busier. I avoid Kat, James, and Steph, their little girl, the best I can. I love them, but it's painful to see what I'm missing.

Today I decide to go by The Java and grab a coffee before I go up to my apartment to study. When I walk through the door, Kat is standing there, holding Steph, with a huge smile on her face. James is behind the counter, and when he sees me, he immediately starts to make my usual drink.

"Throw an extra shot or two in there. I have a late night of studying to do."

"You got it, Bren," James replies.

Kat walks up to me, and I half-hug her since her arms are full. "Hey."

"Hey, yourself. Where have you been? I hardly see you anymore."

"School is kicking my butt this semester. My life consists of school and homework."

"I miss you, Bren. When can we get together and have some girl time?"

I hesitate with my response for a beat, but she catches it. "Well?"

"I don't know, Kat, I feel like I have no time to breathe lately. I suppose after finals next week?"

"Bren, there is something else going on with you, I see it in your eyes. Talk to me."

Saved by the coffee, James barks out my name, and I grab it quickly and wave over my shoulder. "I really have to run. I'm good, Kat. I will see you soon."

I make my way to my apartment, and when I get the door closed behind me, I lean back and sink to the floor. I let go of the breath I was holding, letting the tears slide down my face. I hate that I have created this distance between Kat and myself. I hate that I can't enjoy Steph like I imagined since the day I found out Kat was pregnant during our senior year of high school. I vowed to be there for her, to be by her side every step of the way. But I just can't do it. I can't be around her baby when I don't know if I will ever be able to have one of my own. It hurts my heart too much.

I regain my composure and rise from the floor, only to realize that I have no time to freshen up before I have to leave again. I have an appointment with my specialist in forty-five minutes. I quickly run to the bathroom and splash some water on my face, grab my purse and my lukewarm coffee, and walk back out the door.

I arrive at Dr. Gerrard's office and check in with the receptionist, who gives me a sad smile. I take a seat and am finishing up the last of my cold coffee when I hear my name being called. Once again, I am met with a pity smile, this time from the nurse. I am directed straight to Dr. Gerrard's office instead of an exam room.

"Take a seat; the doctor will be right with you, Bren."

The clock on the wall is ticking loudly, driving me steadily crazier as the seconds pass. I get lost in my own head, thinking of all the things that could be said today. After what seems like hours, when in reality it is only minutes, the door opens, and I am greeted by Dr. Gerrard.

"Hi, Bren, how are you doing today?"

"I'm okay, hoping that I stay that way."

As he rounds his desk and takes a seat, he asks, "Bren, are you sure you want to be here alone? Getting test results and making a plan can be a hard thing. We can wait for your mom or dad to join you."

"Please just tell me what we are looking at and where we go from here. I'm good to handle it whatever it is. I know I have delayed finding out answers and more testing over and over again with rescheduled appointments. I wasn't ready for the answers then."

"Okay, well, with everything that we have looked at, you already know that we have spotted cancer on your right ovary. With the additional testing and biopsies we did last week, we have determined that it has stayed in that area. There hasn't been any spreading to your cervix or uterus. My suggestion to you is that we go ahead with the original surgery plan to remove that ovary, the salpingo-oophorectomy, followed by chemotherapy to make sure all the cancer cells have been removed. Bren, that means that you will lose one ovary and one tube."

I sit, listening to him talk, and a tear starts to slide down my face. "Will I ever be able to have a baby?"

"I want to say yes, but with chemo, and the loss of the one ovary and tube, your likelihood of conception is certainly going to be compromised. I recommend you harvest some eggs to freeze before we move forward. I also want to encourage you to talk to someone. This is not an easy time for you. You are going to need help, especially if you elect surgery. I can't make you to tell anyone, but I want you to know that I think it is a good idea. We have been working together for six months now, and I know you haven't told your family. It was hard enough to get you in here for additional biopsies.

This can be a death sentence and your avoiding the end result isn't helping you any. I think it's now time."

"I will think about it and decide what I want to do. What if I don't opt for surgery? What happens then?"

"The longer you wait to take action, the better chance there is of it spreading, and in that case, you could lose your ability to ever have a child of your own. With all the delayed testing you're lucky you aren't in a worse situation, Bren."

"Thank you, I will give you a call soon to let you know what I've decided."

We say our goodbyes, and I walk out of the office and to my car. When the car door closes, I break down; I can't control my fear and grief any longer.

Look for *Fighting to Save Us Fall 2019*

Acknowledgments

Where do I even begin? After being a reader and then becoming a part of the book world by supporting the self-published authors I love, I took the step to put my own words to paper with the love and support of so many people.

I want to thank my husband Dion and my kids for always supporting me, no matter what. My kids asked, "How are people going to read your book when it's on your computer?" The shock in their face when I say it will be online to buy, and explaining that there will be more than one copy available, was priceless. Thank you to my mom, who has always told me I can do whatever I put my mind to, and I am stronger than I think I am. Thanks also to my family—I love you.

I want to thank my friend Jason Sears, who always pushes me forward, makes me laugh when I need it, and makes me clean my garage when he comes to visit! Now you can say your name is in print.

Thank you to: Melissa Andrea, for being there when I have questions or need your opinion, and for your excitement and support; Tabatha Vargo, the Synopsis Queen; Ella James, for making me feel comfortable with what I was writing and being so supportive and pointing me in the direction of Kiezha, my amazing editor; Kiezha, thank you for doing quality work and then pointing me in the direction of Jamie Davis, who made my book look amazing. I must also thank my beta team leader, Amber Garcia, and team for giving my book a shot and giving me great feedback and suggestions, and Lindee Robinson for an amazing cover and photography. Finally, thank you to Jeannie Christo for being as excited as I am for this book.

Bloggers and reviewers, I want to thank you for taking the time to read and review. You are the ones that help grab the attention of readers, and I appreciate your support in the self-publishing community.

Readers, I must thank you for giving my story a chance, because without you, I wouldn't have anyone besides my family and friends to read my story. I really hope you enjoyed reading my words as much as I enjoyed putting them to paper for you.

Until next time,

Sarah Stevens

About the Author

Sarah Stevens is a New Adult Romance author.

Sarah started writing her first novel The Night He Saved Me in her free time while being a stay-at-home mom. Then one day, it started to flow, and she was writing "The End" in a matter of two months.

When she isn't writing, she is enjoying the southern life with her husband, three kids, a Saint Bernard—who is still adjusting to the southern summers and Bruno a rescue dog. She can't go a day without her coffee in the morning—and a few more cups during the day and her late nights writing.

She enjoys reading Contemporary or New Adult Romance and going to the pool or beach as much as she can. She loves all things Disney and collects Disney mugs to drink her beloved coffee in.

Stay up to date with Sarah's upcoming releases and promotions by signing up for her newsletter: http://eepurl.com/dFwRgb

BookBub: http://bit.ly/2I9xok6
Goodreads: http://bit.ly/2KdNThH

facebook.com/SarahStevensauthor
twitter.com/SarahSAuthor
instagram.com/sarahstevenswrites

www.ingramcontent.com/pod-product-compliance
Lightning Source LLC
LaVergne TN
LVHW051401080426
835508LV00022B/2915